The Ignatian Guide to Forgiveness

Ten Steps to Healing

Marina Berzins McCoy

LOYOLA PRESS.
A JESUIT MINISTRY

Chicago

LOYOLA PRESS.
A JESUIT MINISTRY

3441 N. Ashland Avenue
Chicago, Illinois 60657
(800) 621-1008
www.loyolapress.com

Scripture quotations are from the *New Revised Standard Version Bible: Catholic Edition*, copyright © 1989, 1993 National Council of the Churches of Christ in the United States of America. Used by permission. All rights reserved worldwide.

p. 33 Earthen Vessels, © 1975, 1978, 1991, John B. Foley, SJ, and OCP. All rights reserved.

p. 154 Lord of the Dance, Words: Sydney Carter, © 1963 Stainer & Bell, Ltd. (Admin. Hope Publishing Company, Carol Stream, IL 60188). All rights reserved. Used by permission.

Cover art credit: Praneat/iStock/Getty Images
Back cover author photo, Christopher Soldt Boston College.

ISBN: 978-0-8294-5007-1
Library of Congress Control Number: 2020944539

Printed in the United States of America.
20 21 22 23 24 25 26 27 28 29 Versa 10 9 8 7 6 5 4 3 2 1

For John

Contents

Prologue

The Dance of Forgiveness

Have you ever been to a wedding dance in which the bride and groom dance their first dance together as a married couple, alone out on the dance floor? Soon, the bride and groom each invite a parent or other relative to join the dance, and there are four people dancing. Next, other relatives may join in, until soon everyone is out on the floor. It may be surprising to consider a wedding dance as an image of forgiveness. After all, we think of forgiveness as taking place only between two people. Or we may think of forgiveness mostly in terms of *shoulds* and *oughts*. I may say to myself, *I should forgive this person because God wants me to do so.* Or, *I am required to forgive, because otherwise maybe God will not forgive me.* But forgiveness is not like this. It is much more like a dance, in which our first dance partner is God. But whenever we spend time with God and let God lead us, we are always led back to embrace other people—for example, the one whom we forgive or who forgives us. This forgiveness then gives us the freedom to go and live more generously with others in the wider human family. And then we go on to dance the dance of love with them, too.

Jesus himself uses the image of the wedding hall and the party with invited guests. In the Gospel according to Matthew, Jesus presents God as the host of a huge party where he hopes his invited guests will show up (Matthew 22:1–14). He prepares the best feast for them to enjoy when they arrive. However, many people refuse the invitation. The host of the parable instructs his servants to go out into the street and find new guests. They invite in "both good and bad" until the banquet hall is full. One imagines people from all walks of life: those with money and those without much. People who dress up and those who like to go casual. There are shy people and more outgoing types; those who have many connections and others still finding them. The host does not have an A-list but instead an "all" list; the question is, do we show up to the party?

This story recently resonated with me in a new way, when my husband threw a fiftieth birthday party for me. We invited many friends from a variety of parts of our lives: friends from work, friends from grad-school days, neighbors across the street. My best friend was there, and so was a woman we had not seen since college. When the guests sang "Happy Birthday," I was happy to be surrounded by so many people who represented a variety of times in my life. But in a quieter moment, after the party ended, one of the guests expressed her happiness at being at the party because it brought together people who otherwise might never have met. A friend who was a social worker met an immigration lawyer and hit it off. A single friend enjoyed playing with my neighbor's toddler. My guest's comment helped me realize that the best part of the birthday celebration was really not about me but about all the guests who were present, the community that came about by way of the invitation.

This helped me understand Jesus' parable in a new way and understand forgiveness in a new way too. This parable shows us that God loves to throw a party and to bring together all the people that God loves: rich and poor, fulfilled and struggling, people from all walks of life. Within each person, too, God loves everything that is gifted and beautiful and everything that is broken and flawed. All parts of ourselves are welcome to the party. God wants us to be able to enjoy the feast, cut the cake, listen to music, and get out on the dance floor together. The party is not for God. The party is for us. The celebration is life with God and with one another.

God invites us to come to the celebration. Forgiveness helps us all to get there. God invites us to feast and to dance. Forgiveness is part of how we make our way deeper into the celebration of community and communion, with God and with one another. Forgiveness helps us find our way back into the freedom and giftedness of life.

This book takes up the notion of forgiveness in terms of ten steps we can take toward forgiving others and ourselves. Forgiveness is not really a straight line, however, nor is there a precise method that can bring us from a place of hurt or anger to a place of forgiveness and peace. It is not like taking an antibiotic for an illness. We don't undertake seven days of a regimen and find that we are simply cured. Forgiveness is much more like walking down a winding path, with some difficult areas that are hard to traverse, places where we cannot see what is ahead of the next turn, and then some delightful moments where the path levels out and suddenly the way is easier. When we walk the path closer to forgiveness, we might find that there are times when we have to stop to rest and take a break. Sometimes the road has a fork in it, and we have to choose which way to take, hoping that this path does not have a dead end but brings us to our destination. Sometimes we even have to retrace our steps to an earlier point on the path because we find that we have forgotten something back there and it's too soon to move ahead to the next place. In this way, the journey is more like a meandering dance than a straight line. What matters, though, is that we are on the path.

The ten steps below are offered as a road map. The terrain each one of us travels will have its unique features, specific to each person's dynamics and relationships. For this reason, we need a good guide, one who knows the local area well. Our guide is Jesus. In Scripture, we see that Jesus himself walked the path of forgiveness, offering it to others in his healing ministry, preaching on what it is, and even modeling for us from the cross how to forgive. On the cross, Jesus asks his Father to forgive those who are crucifying him; while he asks his Father to do the work of forgiving, his very desire that those who harm him be forgiven is an act of care for those who have enacted harm (Luke 23:34). In this way, Jesus speaks about forgiveness not simply from the perspective of a divine being but also from the perspective of any human. Jesus makes a good guide for each of us because he knows our inner terrain. He knows what the human landscape looks like inside each of us. Jesus knows us inside and out and has great compassion for the person we are—as well as for the person from whom we are alienated.

Ignatian spirituality provides some excellent resources for allowing God to companion us on the journey. Specific forms of praying, such as the *examen* and imaginative prayer, open up ways for God to communicate with us. Moreover, Ignatius had deep insight into the personal dynamics of spirituality: how we think and feel; how thoughts and feelings can bring us closer to or further away from God; and how prayer can allow God to reshape our vision of ourselves and others. Forgiveness often requires that we delve deeply into our souls and notice what moves them. The philosopher Heraclitus says, "One will never discover the limits of the soul, should one travel every road, so deep a measure does it hold." Ignatius understood the great depths of the soul and how God can assist us in navigating its seemingly unfathomable territory.

The steps below give an outline of what a journey toward forgiveness might look like. At each step, though, we need to rely on God as our personal guide, to allow Jesus' words in Scripture as well as God's communication with us in prayer to bring us closer to our destination. Every person's journey will look a little different because God guides us individually through prayer, reflection, and the gifts God gives us in our everyday world. Ignatian spirituality offers some powerful resources for how to allow God to speak to us individually so that we can be freed to forgive. At each step, there are specific suggestions for how to allow God to enter the unique and personal experience of prayer that can bring us to healing and freedom.

The prophet Isaiah writes,

> Every valley shall be lifted up,
>   and every mountain and hill be made low;
> the uneven ground shall become level,
> and the rough places a plain.

—Isaiah 40:4

God's promise is that while the way forward may seem rugged indeed at first, eventually the landscape will level out. Our destination may not be in sight when we begin the journey, but we have a good companion in Jesus, and so we can travel with hope. When we finally arrive at the banquet hall and join in community with others who have also arrived, the dance at the end is amazing.

A Prayer for Beginning

This prayer is adapted from an ancient prayer said at the end of a pilgrimage Mass for pilgrims along the *Camino de Santiago* ("Way of St. James").[1]

Dear God,
Bless all that we carry with us on this journey, our
      resources and our burdens.
God, you guided the Hebrew people across the
      desert and into the Promised Land.
You sent Jesus to walk alongside his disciples on
      the road.
Watch over us as we walk in your love.
Be our companion on the walk, wisdom in
      our words,
warmth in our hearts, and nourishment in the
      bread we break.
Guide us along the way,
Step by step,
Word by word,
Grace by grace.
In the name of Jesus, Amen.

—adapted by Marina Berzins McCoy

Step One

Find Your Desire

I have walked down the path of forgiveness more than once. Each time, it has been helpful to begin by identifying the answer to this question: What do I want? And then again, what do I *really* want?

Do I want to forgive, or not really? Do I want something else? For example, do I really want an apology? Do I want a relationship back that has been broken and damaged? Maybe I want another person or God to forgive me for my own sinful behavior. Perhaps I desire a deeper healing of a wound inside that continues to ache. Or maybe I want to be free to love others generously, to move on from my own hurt and anger. Sometimes what I have thought I wanted turned out to be different from my deepest desires in the situation. Sometimes my initial desires were not possible because they depended on the actions of another person and so were out of my control. Sometimes I was just being dishonest with myself.

St. Ignatius of Loyola, in his *Spiritual Exercises*, asks that retreatants begin their prayer by asking God for what they desire from that time of prayer. We need to begin with what we desire right now. If my prayer is asking for one thing that I think I "should" want but I really want something else, then prayer is likely to be ineffective. If I go to a store full of healthy food but I really want junk food even though I know that the healthy food is good for me, it is unlikely that I am going to eat well. Instead, I am going to find the one item in the store that is like the junk food I desire—maybe I will talk myself into buying a bag of organic potato chips, when I really need some fresh fruits and vegetables. Until I take an honest look at my own desires, it won't help if there are a hundred nutritious foods around me from which to choose. What matters most is what is going on inside my own mind and heart. What do I think I want? What do I really want? And how are these different?

I can think of a time when I wanted to forgive another person but struggled. A close friend with whom I had shared much of my interior life suddenly abandoned a relationship with me after a conflict. I felt devastated. My trust was shattered. I felt as though I had opened the window of my own soul to another person and he had looked in the window, seen my innermost heart, and then broken the window. Now the shards of glass were mine to pick up. It felt unjust that he had no interest in assisting with the process of repair. He enacted the break, yet I was left to pick up the pieces.

Even after many months, I felt stuck. No matter how much I prayed to be able to forgive and move on, I felt unable to do so. Identifying my own deepest desires helped, although it took a long time to forgive. At first, what I thought I wanted was to forgive so that this other person could move on with his own life and his ministry to others. I genuinely wanted to be a "good Christian" and a good person. But what I *really* wanted at the time, even more, was not to forgive—or at least that was secondary to my other desires. What I wanted most was for this other person to be sorrowful and to repair what was broken. At an even deeper level, I wanted to know that the other person loved me and would make a gesture to express this love and care in our interactions. Instead, there was only silence.

Eventually, I did forgive him. But the first step in forgiveness, for me, had nothing to do with choosing to release my anger or hurt, resolving to be a "good Christian," or deciding to just "move on." The first step was to identify the nature of my own desires and to be honest with myself. When the relationship ended, I did not really want to forgive. I wanted another person to act differently and to show love for me at a time in my life when I felt unloved. I felt shattered, and I wanted wholeness again. What I discovered, much later, was that this other person's care was not, and could never be, the source of my own sense of wholeness. No other person can be the source of genuine self-love. Rather, God's abundant love for me has been the source of my interior healing. Only when this deeper, interior healing took place was I adequately free to let go of my need for the other person's care; this then freed me to forgive.

What are we to do when we discover that our innermost desire after a broken relationship or experience of injustice might not be forgiveness, or at least not *only* forgiveness? What do we do when it turns out that we have deeper desires, or we resist the idea of forgiveness because it seems—and maybe is—so profoundly unfair?

Ignatian spirituality does not tell us to run away from these heartfelt desires or to minimize them. Neither does it suggest that we can make others act in the way that we wish they would act. Only God can convert the heart of another. Instead, the wisdom of Ignatius is to assure us that God wants to meet—and is able to meet—our most heartfelt longings. What I hope to receive from another human being, she or he may not be able to provide. However, God can. God knows our deepest thoughts and feelings. God is able to provide for our deepest longings. When I recognize that God can meet this even deeper desire, then I may be freed up from the need for another to apologize or to do anything differently for me.

For this reason, this book does not focus on reconciliation of relationship, although it is possible that forgiveness can lead to reconciliation. Reconciliation is a beautiful gift when it takes place, and offering forgiveness to another who has hurt us can go a long way toward healing the relationship. But even when reconciliation is refused, forgiveness brings us freedom.

What is the difference between forgiveness and reconciliation? Forgiveness is essentially about the release of anger and pain such that we can again wish another person a good life. Forgiveness frees us to become people who can love again, who can dance the dance of love with God and others. Reconciliation requires forgiveness but goes a step further: It is about the restoration of relationship. In reconciliation, we might go back to a relationship similar to the one that we had before or undertake one that looks completely different. Forgiveness does not always lead to reconciliation, even when we hope for it, because reconciliation requires the participation of another person. Reconciliation can be invited, but the other person also has her own discernment and freedom to forgive or reconcile. Or I might decide that I want to forgive but not resume relationship. In some cases, such as cases of abuse, separating from ongoing relationship might even be the most loving course of action. Forgiveness, however, can still take place. Forgiveness is a process that takes place primarily between God and me. Forgiveness frees.

Our first step on the path is simply to know where we are so that God can meet us there. Where are we beginning? For this is where Jesus wants to meet us. In fact, if you are struggling to forgive another person and you discover that this is not really what you most want, this is good news, not bad! It is good news to discover it and name it, because it may well be that these deeper, unmet desires are the very thing that is holding you back from forgiveness. God wants to meet those desires. That is the good news. Forgiveness does not have all that much to do with another person's sorrow or conversion, although it can be made much easier in these cases. Forgiveness is about better understanding my own desires and my own vulnerability and letting God into these spaces so that God can take care of my needs.

Understanding Our Feelings

Identifying our desires might be easy in some cases, but we do not always understand them immediately. We can begin, however, by asking three basic kinds of questions.

1. First, identify and name your feelings. What feelings are most dominant now? Some feelings that might be present are sadness, anger, grief, shame, resentment, irritation, fear, disgust, rage, contempt, jealousy, distrust, alienation, loneliness, guilt, confusion, anxiety, exasperation, hate, hopelessness, or the sensation of being shattered. It could be that there is a mix of negative and positive emotions, so consider if any of these feelings are also present, even if not all the time: happiness, peace, affection, sympathy, compassion, hope, curiosity, gratitude, tranquility, warmth, understanding, freedom, trust, expectation, or a sense of renewal.

2. Second, notice where and when these feelings arise. What kinds of thoughts or actions lead to feelings of resentment or fear? What kinds of thoughts or actions promote peace or hope?

3. Third, "play detective" with understanding the causes of specific emotions. You might consider what kinds of needs these emotions are communicating. Instead of thinking of feelings as good or bad, think about

emotions as messages that communicate something important.

Let's take an example. Kathleen has been struggling to forgive her ex-boyfriend for breaking off their relationship and for some unkind words that were exchanged between them during the breakup. She is angry that he initially texted her to end the relationship instead of doing it face-to-face. She feels betrayed by this breakup after all the beautiful words he had spoken to her only a few weeks before, expressing his love for her. She can identify feelings of anger, sadness, betrayal, and shame over some of the hurtful words she also said. Kathleen notices that certain thoughts especially increase her feelings of sadness: when she thinks about how he said he did not want to marry her and knew he would never want to marry her, she feels saddest. She also notices that she thinks about her ex-boyfriend the most at the end of the day when she comes home from work and sits alone on the same couch that she used to sit on with him, when she turns on the TV to watch shows they used to watch together. His absence feels most palpable then.

Kathleen starts to realize that along with desiring to forgive her boyfriend for his unkind words and the way he ended the relationship, she also has unmet desires. Some of her desires include knowing that she is attractive and can find a life partner; she also simply wants company at the end of a long day at work. She feels lonely because she does not have someone to spend time with after work. She also feels most upset about the breakup when she thinks about some mistakes she made in the relationship—for example, her tendency to back away from intimacy when she feels as though things are getting too close. Kathleen starts to understand that there are other things going on inside her, along with feeling stuck and unable to forgive. For her, forgiveness may require letting God into her loneliness, feelings of failure, and desires to meet someone who will love her the way she desires to be loved.

Kathleen starts to think about some further choices she wants to make about how she spends her time—for example, getting together with friends some nights after work instead of heading straight for the couch. Identifying her feelings and addressing some of her unmet needs does not lead her straight to forgiveness of her ex-boyfriend, but for her it is an important first step.

As we walk toward forgiveness, one of the earliest steps can be to practice identifying our emotions and offering them to God. We might even feel very strong emotions toward God—such as anger at God for letting the harm happen. God is strong enough to receive any emotion: sadness, disappointment, resentment, and even anger or sadness directed at God. God loves us and wants to receive all of who we are, right now, today.

What do you feel, and what would it mean to share these feelings openly with God?

Lord, I yearn for
rest
embrace
relief
release
peace
home.

Sometimes I am tempted by
cynicism
fatigue
skepticism
resentment
doubt
despair.

Grant me your grace, and help me to grow in
strength
generosity
courage

maturity
gratitude
joy.

Some of the above ideas come from the insights of cognitive behavioral therapy (CBT): how we think affects how we feel, and we can shape how we feel in part by changing how we think. Understanding these connections has great value and can give us further insight into what is happening inside when we struggle to forgive. If I can identify and challenge my thought processes, I may be freed up to forgive. Ignatius recognized many of the core ideas of CBT, such as the centrality of the relationship between thoughts and feelings and needing to discern the difference between those thoughts and feelings that lead us closer to well-being and those that do not.[2] But Ignatian spirituality goes even deeper than CBT in its exploration of desire. *My deepest desires are not identical to my strongest feelings.* Ignatius recognized that how we feel is not only about a link between thoughts and emotions, although Ignatius also had profound insight into these kinds of psychological connections. Moreover, I am not the only one with desires and aims in my life. God also has hopes, dreams, and desires for me.

Consolation and Desolation

Ignatius noticed that our patterns of thoughts and feelings can reveal how God is drawing us toward God's greatest hopes and desires for us and whether we are either going along with God's desires for us or resisting. Our lives have a purpose and meaning. God communicates with us about the direction of our lives through gentle interior movements, by how we feel. These feelings also require reflection. By paying close attention to our interior experiences when we pray, we can learn to listen to what God wants to communicate. God wants us to grow into people who are more loving, free, and generous. Prayer, as well as action, helps us become loving, free, and generous people.

Ignatius thought that we could better understand where God is present in our lives by understanding two main kinds of movements in the soul: *consolation* and *desolation*. Consolation exists when we are being led closer and closer to God and toward love of other people. Consolation exists when we are full of energy to praise, to love, and to serve God and others. In consolation, we are drawn outside of ourselves to others. When I am in consolation, I am eager to love others, to leave behind my own petty concerns, and to be more available and generous with a wider community of people. Desolation is a sign that I am moving further away from God.

Desolation exists when I feel closed in on myself, trapped or unfree, and preoccupied with myself rather than open to a wider world.

God leads us through consolation. God prefers the "carrot" to the "stick" in encouraging us to move forward on our life's path. This is true even when we are stuck in difficult patterns and don't know how to get out of them. Like a loving parent who would rather help her child leave behind a dangerous piece of glass on the playground by calling the child over to a new spot and something wonderful to be explored, God lures us on toward new life through attraction. However, we often act like little children in response to God's parenting, and we might resist. I might insist on wanting to play with the piece of broken glass, even if I know it is not good for me. For example, when I felt that my trust was shattered, one of the ways God drew me away from hurt was to bring my attention to other relationships of love and care in my life. Staying overly focused on my thoughts and feelings of broken trust was not the direction God wanted me to go. Ignatian spirituality teaches us to better understand what is happening inside us when we are attracted to what is life giving or what can harm us. Then we are better able to discern where God is leading.

Jesus is clear throughout Scripture that God desires forgiveness and reconciliation. But getting to forgiveness is not as simple as gritting our teeth and choosing to forgive. Rather, to forgive often requires sorting out, with God's help, complex inner dynamics and feelings. Ignatian spirituality helps us sort through our feelings and experiences so that we can better understand what to follow and what to walk away from. When Jesus calls the disciples who are fishermen in the Gospel accounts, he tells them, "Follow me, and I will make you fish for people" (Matthew 4:19). And the disciples put down their nets to follow. Some of our own obstacles to forgiveness are like nets that trap us. Paying attention to consolation and desolation helps us get out from under these nets, put them down, and follow the Lord to where he wants to take us.

Consolation and desolation are not identical with positive and negative emotions. A person can feel good but be desolate, as when he is engaged in unhealthy thrill seeking, substance abuse, or other kinds of addictions. There may be short-term energy, but in the long term we are being led away from love, freedom, and interior peace. We can also experience consolation even when we feel bad—for example, when experiencing grief. When my husband's grandparents died, I was overwhelmed with grief and cried uncontrollably in the church pew during the service. They had been like my own family. However, I also felt deeply connected to my husband and his relatives. I felt grateful that I had known his grandparents and that they had treated me with the same love as they gave their own grandchildren. I recalled memories of being invited into their home when I was first dating my husband and on a long road trip to visit him over the college summer break. Their house was partway through the trip, and they invited me to stay in their guest room. I remembered the delicious pancakes his grandparents fed me at breakfast, and the way they made me feel so welcome, even though they had never met me. These memories also led to a desire for me to be comforting and kind to my husband and his parents after the funeral. Although I was sad, the overall experience was one of increased connection, love, and gratitude: consolation.

Ignatius offers a specific form of prayer that helps us notice the larger patterns of consolation and desolation and to recognize where God is present in our lives: the *examen*. Through the *examen*, we start with our feelings and naming them and then move to understanding how God wants us to respond to our feelings and experiences. God has hopes and desires for us that are sometimes bigger than we can imagine. The *examen* helps us understand our feelings and desires and also where God is leading us in them and through reflection upon them.

The Examen

First, I place myself in the presence of God and begin with a sense of being known and loved by God. For example, I might imagine Jesus looking at me with love, or I might imagine God's love for me as akin to warm sunshine. I express gratitude to God for this love.

Second, I ask God to help me to see where God's love and life have been present in my life and to be honest with God and with myself in this time of prayer. I need God's insights and not only my own to better understand the experiences that I bring to prayer.

Third, I review the day in God's presence, noticing where I experienced consolation and where I experienced desolation. Where was I loving, and where did I struggle to love? If I am struggling with forgiveness, I might specifically review where there has been peace, healing, or greater reconciliation and where I still have difficulties. I might notice moments when I have felt freedom, peace, and renewal in my relationships or life and where I still feel a lack of freedom.

Fourth, I bring one element of this experience into conversation with God. I speak to God about it and wait for a response, either in words or in insights or feelings.

Last, I consider the next day and where God might be leading me to act next.

In my experience of the *examen*, I've found that it is important not to pray *only* over the broken relationship or situation in need of forgiveness, even though this may be very tempting when it is my focus. It is more helpful to pray over the whole of one's day and *all the places that God is present.* God may be using gifts in other areas of life to draw us into new life and forgiveness of the old. For example, Kathleen might find that paying attention to the care that her brothers and sisters have shown her reminds her that she has other relationships of love in her life. The relationship of the past is still in need of healing as she finds her way to forgiveness, but it is set in the context of a larger set of relationships and experiences of family and community.

Here is a simple example of what an *examen* might look like in a time of struggling with forgiveness. In this case, Mary is upset at a coworker, Bill, who constantly belittles her contributions and those of others at the office. She struggles to forgive Bill, but because his behavior continues and her supervisor is unsympathetic, she feels stuck. Today, when Mary presented a new budget proposal, Bill treated it dismissively in front of Mary's peers. Although others thought it a good idea and the budget was accepted, Bill's comments still nag at her.

Jesus, please be present to me. Let me know that you are really here with me, listening as a friend while I review the day. I am so grateful to you for the many gifts in my life. My heart is aching a bit today, but I remember that you love me. Even now, I can see you looking at me with warmth and affection. Help me understand the situation and myself better.

My day started off pretty well, and I enjoyed breakfast with my husband and children. I packed the kids some lunch, and although Tommy complained about having apples again, I didn't mind and put a tangerine in there instead for him. I felt lucky and grateful that my kids are generally good kids and are willing to tell me what they like me to pack them for lunch. My husband gave me a sweet hug and kiss on the way out the door. I felt full of good energy for the day ahead.

When I arrived at work, I felt pleased with the way this new budget would help our business to negotiate some recent challenges. I worked hard on it and had some good feedback from my supervisor. But then a coworker who always cuts down my work made a snide comment about the budget I had worked on for this project, in front of others. I felt hurt and angry, and a little humiliated. After that, I just stopped talking in the meeting, and the rest of the day at work I kept thinking about what he said. Other people complimented the work I had done, but I came home tired and cranky. When I picked up the kids, one of them brought out a picture of a snowman to put on the fridge. I said something nice quickly and put it on the fridge but was so tired that I ignored him a bit. When I unpacked the lunch boxes, I saw that the tangerine went uneaten. After dinner, we watched a TV show, and I laughed really hard at this episode. But now, as I come to pray, I feel sad again.

What I most want to bring to you is the incident with Bill. I want to let go of my hurt and to forgive him, but he never changes. He is so insensitive. I don't know what to do, as I have asked him to not say hurtful things, but he stays the same, and our supervisor does not seem to care. I don't want to leave this job; I love it most of the time. What should I do?

I sit in silence a little while and wait for God. I don't hear any words in prayer, but I feel a sense of warmth and comfort arise in the center of my body, and a feeling that God understands what I have experienced. I realize that this comment from my coworker was the second time I was told that what I was offering was "not good enough." When my child complained about the apple, I was able to take it in stride, but with my colleague, there is a whole, longer history of negativity. I was reacting not just to the one comment but also to all the other comments he has made in the past. It occurs to me that my coworker is like this with everyone in my department. It is not specific to me. There must be something going on deep inside of him, and his response has nothing to do with me in particular. I still feel hurt by the experience, but maybe I can let go of personalizing his comments so much. It's not about me. I wonder what made Bill into this kind of a person who feels the need to belittle others. I feel a little sorry for him.

I decide that when I see Bill, I will be warm and smile and accept his reaction, whether he is responsive and kind in return or not. I will try to remember that you, Jesus, appreciate my attempts to be kind and generous to others whether or not he does. If he is negative, I will take a moment or two to bring to mind my husband's warm hug and let that be my comfort in the middle of the day. And, oh yes, tomorrow I will be sure to compliment my child's picture of the snowman, because I let that gift of the day get past me, and I would like him to know that his gift of care was appreciated.

The example above concerns a relatively common and straightforward case of a hard-to-forgive crabby colleague. Other situations, such as the breakup of a long-term romantic partnership or the loss of a job, can have many more dimensions. These take time to work through with God's assistance. The advantage of the *examen* is that, if we pray it daily, we do not have to work through *all* the dimensions of the situation at once and arrive at a resolution. Instead, we can let just a single day's thoughts, feelings, and experiences slowly help us find where God is leading us as we move closer to forgiveness. We can allow God to work with us slowly through each day's experiences as they happen. God shows us longer-term patterns that help us see where God is leading us. God also gives us the little steps that we can take in order to follow God more closely.

Praying the *examen* will also help us better understand what we want. For instance, Mary thought she wanted Bill to be nicer to her. She did want this, but then she realized an even deeper desire, which was to feel that her contributions at work were valuable and to feel loved and appreciated. Praying helped Mary remember other people in her life who do love and appreciate her, such as her husband and child, and to recall that God's love is always there for her. Bill may or may not change, but the *examen* allows Mary to see where God is guiding her to place her energy, in ways that will likely also promote her capacity to forgive.

By praying the *examen*, over time we can start to discover more about our own desires and about God's deepest desires for us, the first step on the path toward forgiveness.

Step Two

Embrace Being a Creature and Name Your Inner Pharisee

Forgiving another person also brings us face-to-face with a deeply philosophical and spiritual question: Are human beings worthy of love only for their gifts and virtues or even with their faults and sins? Does God love us in our wholeness? Can we love human beings in their wholeness too? Do I love *myself* only when I am good, or can I really embrace that I am lovable in all my humanity? This embrace of my own humanity often leads me to become more able to embrace others in theirs. When I know that God loves me "as is," I can love myself as I am. When I love myself as I am, while remaining honest with myself about my own limits, I learn increasingly to love others in their wholeness too.

In the story of the creation of Adam, the first human being, God creates him out of a mixture of dust and divine breath. We are like Adam—and like Eve, who was taken from Adam's flesh, right near the rib cage where this divine breath first flowed and mixed with his dustiness. We are all a mixture of dust and divine breath. We possess a mixture of talents and limits, gifts and deficiencies, and yet God's Spirit flows through it all.

Ignatius of Loyola's *Spiritual Exercises* begin with the experience of being a "loved sinner." In the four weeks of the Exercises for a person undertaking a thirty-day retreat, the theme of the first week is to know that one is sinful and in need of redemption and yet is deeply loved. Ignatius begins here because it is through this experience of knowing that one sins and yet is still deeply loved that one comes to better understand what it means to live in friendship with God.

How can we concretely find our way forward to loving human beings in their wholeness? One way is by spending some time reflecting on one of Jesus' parables, which gives us some helpful imagery with which to pray. Ignatius encouraged us to use our imaginations as we pray. When we enter a Gospel scene by letting it play out in our imagination, we allow God room to continue to communicate with us. God did not speak only to Abraham and Moses. God continues to speak to us, too, in the most interior spaces of our hearts when we pray with our imaginations.

The Parable of the Lost Sheep

Jesus' parable of the lost sheep gives us an image of a God who loves us and seeks us out, no matter how lost we are. In Luke's Gospel, Jesus says in Luke 15:4–7:

> Which one of you, having a hundred sheep and losing one of them, does not leave the ninety-nine in the wilderness and go after the one that is lost until he finds it? When he has found it, he lays it on his shoulders and rejoices. And when he comes home, he calls together his friends and neighbors, saying to them, "Rejoice with me, for I have found my sheep that was lost." Just so, I tell you, there will be more joy in heaven over one sinner who repents than over ninety-nine righteous persons who need no repentance.

I volunteer in a men's prison in Massachusetts. In the small library where we sometimes meet, there is a poster of Jesus as a shepherd, rescuing a sheep from a dangerous ledge on which it has become trapped. Jesus is at the edge of a cliff, reaching down with a muscular arm to rescue the sheep at considerable risk to himself. In this picture, he looks like a burly man. One of the men, whom I will call Scott, once remarked that there is nothing weak in this image of Jesus. Jesus is both vulnerable and strong, willing to take risks for the sake of the wayward sheep. Scott could identify with the experience of being sought out by a Jesus whose courage and strength were as significant as his gentleness and kindness. Scott said, "I learned from Jesus that to forgive others, I had to know that Jesus forgave me first. I also learned that it is not weak but strong to forgive." Scott's comment is right on point. To forgive often requires courage and a willingness to take risks. Forgiveness is not weakness but rather a courageous choice to face human complexity and to embrace the risk involved in loving what is human. Moreover, to forgive, we need to soften our hearts and develop compassion for others. This compassion to forgive often comes from embracing that we, too, are loved sinners, in need of forgiveness.

This is not always easy. A man I will call Tom shared with our prison group how he struggled to forgive his brother. A couple of times a year, his brother would write Tom to ask him for forgiveness for a serious past wrong. Tom himself was in prison for a crime and, after repenting, believed that God forgave his past. Yet Tom still struggled to forgive his brother for his wrongdoing. He knew that there was something inconsistent here: how could he accept God's love and forgiveness and yet not offer it? Yet he admitted to the group, quite honestly, that it was hard to offer forgiveness to his brother. Tom's honesty with himself is a good model for us. He courageously identified his feelings and desires and yet also started to wonder whether he wanted to go further toward repairing this broken family relationship.

When Jesus tells the parable of the lost sheep and the shepherd who goes to find it, it is immediately after the Pharisees have criticized Jesus for talking and eating with sinners and tax collectors (Luke 15:1–2). This parable is his response to them. Jesus' parable is also a response to the inner Pharisee in each one of us.

We might not immediately identify with the Pharisees or the teachers of the law; after all, they can sound like historical figures from long ago. But in undertaking a process of forgiveness, it can be useful to find my inner Pharisee. The Gospel writers who include this story likely recognized that this attitude of judgment toward the sinner was not limited to a small group of religious leaders who objected to Jesus. Many of us have a side to ourselves that is akin to the Pharisee whether we want to admit it or not! One step toward forgiveness is to find out how and where we are like those who objected to Jesus' love of sinners. What parts of us are harsh and judgmental, more concerned with rules or the protection of institutions than with the reconciliation of broken relationships? What part of me offers judgment or self-judgment, when God's call is for compassion? What part of me really doesn't like the "creatureliness" of myself or others?

Embracing Our Creatureliness

In his parable, Jesus uses the image of a large flock of sheep: one hundred sheep. Jesus does not describe just one lost sheep returned to a shepherd but rather a lost sheep returned to an entire *community* of sheep. We human beings are those sheep! Jesus repeatedly uses this image of the shepherd and sheep to describe his relationship to us: in John's Gospel, Jesus is described as the "good shepherd [who] lays down his life for the sheep" (John 10:11). Jesus is the shepherd who leads his flock and knows each one of his sheep by name.

I have not always found this image of sheep to be entirely pleasant. I grew up on a small piece of farmland where the house was rented to my mother and stepfather. My brother and I used to enjoy running around on the fields; we lived in an area with no sidewalks and not a lot of other children but enjoyed the proximity of a barn, barn cats, chickens, and occasionally other animals. For a while, our landlord owned three sheep. Sheep are not always like the cute little lambs we see on prayer cards, held in Jesus' arms with clean, sparkling-white wool. Sheep are animals. Sometimes they are cute and adorable, but their wool can also get dirty. Sheep smell. Sheep are also not known for being especially bright; for this reason, they can easily go astray and lose their way back to the flock. When my brother and I used to pet the sheep near our home, our fingers would be left with a sticky lanolin residue afterward. My mother always reminded us to wash our hands to remove the germs when we came back indoors. I remember many years ago when my first Jesuit spiritual director recommended that I pray with the image of being one of the sheep that Jesus "knows by name." When I did, the idea was profoundly uncomfortable to me. I did not want to be this grungy, dirty, dumb creature. Where was the dignity in it? My director gently reminded me that we are creatures. What would it mean to embrace my "creature-liness"? he asked.

In a way, we all have this choice: to remain with our inner Pharisee and separate what is limited in others and ourselves or to listen to Jesus and embrace being a creature of God. Jesus' parable draws our attention to the creatureliness of ourselves and others. We are creatures and not the Creator. We are made in the *image* of God, and so we are holy, but we are also embodied, finite, limited, and sometimes sinful. Sometimes our coats get grungy and gray. Sometimes we go astray. Yet in Jesus' eyes we are also that adorable, cuddly, beloved sheep. Jesus wants to snuggle with us. Jesus comes for us with love. Jesus not only comes to bring home the lost sheep but also emphasizes the joy in the reunion: "When he has found it, he lays it on his shoulders and rejoices" (Luke 15:5).

Pope Francis has spoken to priests of the need to be "shepherds living with 'the smell of the sheep.'"[3] But all of us, laypeople as well as priests and religious, are called to be this kind of shepherd. We can be good shepherds precisely because we are also lost sheep who have been found. We can forgive because we realize that we are those smelly yet adorable and adored sheep, who have needed to be rescued from ourselves sometimes. None of us is fundamentally different from any other human being insofar as we are all creaturely, all imperfect, and all *beloved* in our imperfection. This does not mean that we ought not strive to become better people or assist others in their personal and spiritual growth. It means that holiness is not the condition for being loved. Loving and being loved "as is" is what encourages us to become holier.

In Jesus' day, sharing a meal with others had many rules built around it. For example, Jewish people and Samaritans had different dietary laws, which meant that they did not typically share meals. Today, also, eating together is about more than the consumption of food for the body. To share a meal means to participate in a common life, to share in moral and spiritual traditions. Sharing a meal means sharing in community. The Pharisees objected to sharing a meal with a sinner, out of a wish for the protection of the community. After all, the sinner might be a dangerous or corrupting force! But we also exclude people from relationship within our own communities, whether the table is the Thanksgiving table, the table at church where we share in the Eucharist and worship together, or other spaces where we are divided.

A step on the path to forgiveness is to embrace the creatureliness of self and others. Then we are better prepared to sit down at the same table and break bread with one another again. There are several ways to pray that can help.

1. Name your inner judgment maker. Most of us are more easygoing in some aspects of life but, in other areas, are more judgmental and have more severe expectations of right and wrong. In what situations are you most likely to judge people harshly? Are there certain categories of people whom you hold to especially high standards?

2. Pray imaginatively with the image of the shepherd seeking out the lost sheep. Begin by rereading the passage

from Luke's Gospel above. Imagine yourself as the lost person, separated from Jesus, the good shepherd. What are you wearing? What does the landscape look like? What sights, sounds, or smells do you notice? Imagine Jesus as he approaches you to find you, pull you up, and embrace you. What does Jesus look like in his expression and gestures when he finds you? What does it feel like to be embraced and brought back to the community of other sheep? Pay special attention to moments of "consolation," when peace, love, or gratitude are awakened.

3. On another occasion, pray with this passage again. This time, imagine that the person you are seeking to forgive is the lost sheep. Walk alongside Jesus, or imagine that you are seeing the scene through Jesus' eyes. What does the other person look like from this point of view? What is Jesus feeling and experiencing as he searches for the lost sheep? How does Jesus feel when he finds him or her? When the other person returns to the community, what does Jesus experience as he observes this scene of reunion?

4. What other image or images help you to understand yourself as a creature made by God in love and cherished by God as a creature? Some images Jesus uses to

name God's care for what is finite and limited include a
flower in the field; a bird in the air; grass in a field; the
salt of the earth; a light from a lamp; a child asking for
a piece of bread; or a fruitful tree. What other images
speak to you about the goodness of being created?

Earthen Vessels

Light has shown in our darkness
God has shown in our heart
With the light of the glory
Of Jesus the Lord

Refrain: We hold a treasure, not made of gold,
In earthen vessels, wealth untold
One treasure only, the Lord, the Christ
In earthen vessels.

He has chosen the lowly,
Who are small in this world;
In his weakness is glory,
In Jesus the Lord.

—John Foley, SJ
© 1975, John Foley and OCP

Step Three

Honor Anger but Deepen Compassion

When we struggle to forgive, our primary emotions may include anger and resentment. Paradoxically, one of the least helpful things in releasing anger is to simply tell ourselves, *Don't feel angry!* Anger has a legitimate place among human emotions. It even has a legitimate place in the process of forgiveness. Yet how often we believe that if we are good Christians, we ought to push away this anger or try to overcome it through the sheer force of will. This rarely works.

Honoring Our Own Anger

I can remember when I was struggling with my anger over a past experience of abuse by a family member. Although I had relatively limited contact with him as an adult, I received a phone call that renewed my distress and reminded me of why I had placed limits on this relationship in the first place. I went to my spiritual director, assuming that he would tell me to release my anger and maybe even give me some prayers that would help me to stop it. After all, the worst of my experiences took place many years before, and yet here they were again, like a roaring wave in the wake of a ship that had long ago departed. Instead, he said, "Reverence your anger." Reverence? For my anger? But I wanted to forgive and move on. Yet my director was right. What I most needed at that point was to honor my anger, for in doing so, I was also reverencing what was holy and good in me that had been harmed. By honoring my anger, I was also able to consider what kinds of choices I could make that would help me feel safe enough to forgive.

Anger is compatible with justice and even compatible with a longer process of forgiveness. We have a model for how this takes place in Jesus. Jesus expresses anger when he sees God's temple being treated like a marketplace, and he turns over the tables of the moneylenders and salesmen (Matthew 21:12; Mark 11:15; Luke 19:45; John 2:15–16). Jesus sees that there is injustice in God's house. Jesus does not shy away from his emotion of anger. As Fr. James Martin, SJ, writes, "Jesus' anger is always a righteous anger, never on behalf of himself, but in reaction to how he sees others being treated. . . . Jesus' anger is, in a word, unselfish and constructive, intent on doing something, effecting a change."[4]

Anger is part of our creatureliness. We are human, and as human beings we are given the gift of many emotions. Some of these emotions, such as anger or fear, may not always feel like gifts because they are unpleasant to experience. Still, they communicate to us that something is amiss, either within us or in our world. Anger can then be good, for it can give us energy and motivation to change unjust structures. Forgiveness does not always require giving up the pursuit of justice. Where injustices are ongoing and systemic, or will lead to future harm of others, then forgiveness without justice would mean a failure to love others. For example, anger at an institution that we love, such as the church in its past failures to prevent sexual abuse, can be part of our love for the Body of Christ. The desire that the church change for the better can motivate action that leads to constructive behavior, such as working for new guidelines to protect children.

Still, anger has its limits, and when we embark on the path of forgiveness, the aim is to release anger and resentment in the long run. Anger can also lead us to act in ways that are not well discerned. Anger may be a strong motivator, but it is usually not a very good guide for making well-thought-out decisions about how to act. Anger activates an animal part of our neurology, leading us perhaps to act impulsively. Ongoing anger can consume our energy so that we are unable to use our energies for other purposes. Even if anger is justified, it may be the case that this anger limits how well I can undertake the other kinds of projects that God desires for me to pursue. If I am angry about injustice all the time and cannot ever let go of these feelings, I will likely be limited in my capacity to love others in everyday life.

Deciding how to act in response to anger is a matter of prayerful discernment. How can we respond to anger in a way that is in keeping with God's desire that we be loving persons? How can we embrace anger while still pursuing the path of forgiveness?

First, we can follow the advice of my former director and *honor* our anger. Second, we can hold intense anger without acting on it until it dissipates or transforms into something else. Anger, disappointment, fear, and other such emotions naturally soften if we simply stay with them and hold them. Thich Nhat Hanh, a Buddhist spiritual leader, suggests that we hold our pain like a baby.[5] If one of us had a baby who was crying and hurt, we would try to comfort the baby, not ignore or harm him. Similarly, we can imagine our anger to be like an upset baby and hold and comfort ourselves with compassion for our anger. Third, when our anger has dissipated, we can come back to the feeling of anger and notice what caused it and then decide how to respond. For example, consider anger that arises from a serious political injustice. There might be many feelings in that anger to sort out. I am the child of refugees, so when I see mistreatment of immigrants, I feel especially angry because I identify my family's experience with the situation before me. If I can sit with my anger before making decisions about how to respond to it, I can be more in touch with the roots of these feelings. Then I can make decisions about what to do with the feelings, such as work for laws that I think are better, or engage in nonviolent protest of bad laws to exhibit support for the immigrants who live in my diverse city.

Feelings are an aspect of our creatureliness. Feelings in themselves are not good or bad, but it is how we respond to them that matters. When in the grip of powerful emotions such as anger, imagine holding these feelings like a baby in your arms until they settle. Then add to the picture: imagine God's loving arms surrounding you and the baby, holding and strengthening both of you.

Prayer in a Time of Anger

God of welcome, God of embrace,
As ocean waves rise and fall,
as stormy clouds gather and clear,
as moving winds blow and subside,
So, too, does my anger move me.
Be my raft in stormy waters,
my stable rock, and my gentle breeze.
Receive and hold my feelings until they subside.
Grant me patience to withstand the waves,
peace to replace the turmoil, and
discernment to know how to respond in love and
        freedom.
Amen

—Marina Berzins McCoy

Deepening Compassion

It is not enough to care for our anger and hurt, however, if
we want to forgive. In order to forgive, we must also deepen
our compassion. Compassion is a matter of the imagination.
When we can imagine another person differently, we may be
able to grow in compassion for the other.

In Ignatius's *Spiritual Exercises*, he often asks us to imagine
the life and death of Jesus to better understand what Jesus
experienced. By using our imagination to enter Jesus' world,

we also give God space to enter our most interior selves to continue communicating God's self to us and to teach us something new. Ignatian imaginative prayer is like a door that gives us access to Jesus' life. We can walk into Jesus' world, even today! But this door also opens the other way, and it creates an interior room into which God also enters—our hearts. When we pray using the imagination, we take a step toward letting God in to witness and be with us in our suffering or confusion. A fundamental step in spiritual maturity is understanding that no other person except God will witness the whole of a person's life. Yet God's witness of our lives is not distant or from above but intimate and from within. God sees and understands all of who we are.

When we have a more personal understanding of Jesus' way of living, we also grow in friendship with him. Jesus' acts of forgiveness and mercy are not merely rules for action that we are to follow because God said so. Jesus' life of compassion and reconciliation shows us what it is like to live a life that is *fully human*. When we imagine what Jesus experienced and allow God's grace to affect our imaginative prayer, we allow God to help us reimagine what it means to be human.

Jesus' clearest testimony about forgiveness is when he himself forgives those who are crucifying him. He says, "Forgive them; for they know not what they are doing" (Luke 23:34).

Jesus' words humble me. Not only is Jesus still being crucified as he utters these words, but also his torturers have expressed no remorse. They are not sorry for what they are doing. There is no clear indication that later, after his death, they will be sorrowful either. Many of Jesus' friends have abandoned him. Nevertheless, Jesus extends forgiveness to all of them. When he asks his Father to offer them forgiveness, this is not only divine compassion at work but also an example of how we can live an authentically human life. Already, by asking God to forgive, Jesus is undertaking his own process of forgiveness in extending care for those who harm him.

At one level, Jesus' response might inspire a degree of resistance. Many philosophers who work on the nature of forgiveness suggest that forgiveness is not necessary or even good until the one who does harm has expressed remorse. I might think that another person ought to be sorry before he or she "deserves" forgiveness. I may say that I will forgive only if it seems fair to forgive. But the great challenge to this way of thinking is that this is not how Jesus himself acts. He does not wait for remorse. He does not wait for the soldiers or for his friends to "get it." It is understandable for us to desire that those who have hurt us understand how we feel and show remorse, but Jesus' example shows us that this is not the only way forward. Jesus shows us a way forward that is freer.

Forgiveness and Ignorance

We have only a few words from Jesus to work with, to explain why he is so free to forgive. But those few words are crucially insightful: "They know not what they do." Jesus does not ask for any conditions to be met before he forgives. For example, he does not ask that the soldiers express sorrow, quit their jobs, change their characters, or even stop crucifying him. Instead, he simply forgives, with the explanation that those who harm him do not know what they are doing. These soldiers do not appear to know Jesus personally. They do not understand the nature of Jesus' ministry or teaching or how he is participating in God's redemptive work. In some ways, they do not fully see the humanity of the person they are torturing—or else they would not do it. Jesus recognizes that in many situations when we harm one another, we are profoundly ignorant of what we are doing.

This is mostly true of those who harm us as well. They "do not know what they are doing." Even if a person knows the *action* that he or she is doing, *how we see or experience* that action might not be fully known. Judgments sometimes cloud the human capacity for empathy. The soldiers who killed Jesus may have been thinking, "But he is a criminal." This identification of Jesus with the criminal led them to think they were enacting justice instead of doing harm. They did not recognize that he was the Messiah, sent to bring love and salvation. Many philosophers of forgiveness suggest that if we do not know the full extent of what we are doing in harming another, we are not culpable. But the situation is complicated; it is common for us to be unaware of how we are harming others, and it's just as common for those who hurt us not to fully understand how, or to what extent, they are harming us. We are creatures of compassion, yet we never know another's experience completely from that person's perspective. This helps me in extending forgiveness to others: perhaps their actions include a degree of not fully knowing or understanding what is at stake for me in how I experience their action or inaction.

Fear can also limit our compassion. Jesus' friends *did* know and love him, and they could see what was wrong, but some of them were afraid. They reacted to his suffering out of fear. Peter promised Jesus that he would stay by his side no matter what, but then he fled out of fear for himself. Many of Jesus' other friends also fled out of fear or confusion.

Often, when we hurt others or are hurt by them, so much of our experience of the event is unknown to anyone else involved. For example, when another person hurts us by ending a relationship that we have treasured, we might not know

- the person's reasons or motivation for ending the relationship
- the other person's internal experience of the breakup (is she as sad as I am? missing me? relieved? or as happy as can be?)
- whether they now value or will later value memories of the relationship
- whether they understand and have compassion for how I feel about it
- how their life experiences and history led them to act in this way

We may also think it obvious that our side of events is clear and easy to understand, justifiable, and maybe even irrefutably true. But our experience may not be fully understood by the other person, no matter how much we attempt to communicate or explain it.

The situation is not always that different when a relationship remains intact. For example, consider Jeff and Julie. They are brother and sister and had a profound conflict in the aftermath of their mother's death. Julie lived closer to her mother when she was ill and so ended up doing a significant portion of the caregiving. Jeff offered some financial assistance and flew in twice to help out but was not able to do much in the way of day-to-day care. Julie and Jeff had different perspectives on their situation. Julie resented that she had done as much of the caregiving as she had; Jeff felt that he was not in a realistic position to do more and that Julie had never communicated clearly her need for more help. Moreover, Jeff felt a degree of loss at not being present when his mother died and felt that Julie had shared some sacred moments with their mother that he had not been able to experience. While they had shared their perspectives with each other, they never saw eye to eye about the situation. But with a long history between them, they shared a familial love that endured. Part of their reconciliation was coming to understand that they would never see the situation identically but that this was okay. They each could live with the other's lacking a bit in understanding the past. Their care for each other was deeper than the desire to be understood, and their understanding of each other in other shared experiences became more important than this one past conflict.

Jesus models for us something truly remarkable. *Although he is the one being harmed, he develops empathy and compassion for the one who wronged him.* Forgiveness and reconciliation always rely to some degree on a capacity to feel compassion and empathy for those who harm us. During his crucifixion, Jesus feels compassion for his friends and for the soldiers alike, even though they do not fully understand the impact of their actions.

Compassion is really a matter of developing our imaginations. Forgiveness and reconciliation are often about finding our way into imagining the unimaginable. In the musical *Hamilton*, Alexander and his wife, Eliza, reconcile after the death of their child, after Alexander's infidelity to Eliza. In the song "It's Quiet Uptown," Angelica sings about how we often find that words can fail to name our experience of forgiveness and transformation, because grace is even more powerful than the words that we can put to our experience. Angelica says that we can too easily reject that which we find to be "unimaginable." The word "unimaginable" develops over the course of the song: for some people, looking on at Alexander and Eliza, it is unimaginable that they could reconcile after Eliza has been publicly humiliated by Alexander's cheating. It is also unimaginable for others to understand what it is like to grieve the loss of a child. No one can truly imagine what they are going through. Yet grace allows what is unimaginable to happen, for love to break through human limits and make real what has been beyond imagination. Alexander and Eliza reconcile. Grace allows us to reimagine the unimaginable, often by giving new shape to relationships through a process of grief and the regrowth of love after pain and betrayal.

While I experienced much family love growing up, one of the adults in my extended family sometimes acted in ways that were hurtful. He was never capable of understanding that his actions were problematic, even when he was directly confronted. As an adult, it became more important that I forgive him than cling to pain and anger. In a way, my decision to forgive was rooted in a moment early in my childhood when I considered how I wanted to live. I can think of a particular moment, standing in a parking lot when I was only about five or six years old. I had been acting up a bit inside the store, and when we left, he pulled me over to a stranger in the parking lot and said something about me that felt cruel and humiliating. The stranger hurried away, not wanting to get involved in another family's emotional drama. Although I was very young, I could recognize that what he did was not good. I made the decision on the spot that I would not grow up to be like him when I became an adult. Even as a child, I was able to see that my family member did not "know" what he was doing—despite the fact that he was the adult and I was the child!

Yet it was only my adult self that learned compassion, through discovering more about that relative's personal history—including some profound suffering in his own childhood. I learned to see that he, too, was a lovable yet wounded person who had endured some experiences that I could never imagine; for example, he endured acts of violence from others in the city in which he lived when he was only a child. Moreover, I have sometimes struggled with my own emotional self-regulation, not always in the same ways he did but rather in ways that reminded me that we all struggle with our emotions at times. The development of my compassion had nothing to do with any changes in my relative. He never did change and remained rather consistently himself throughout his life: funny and generous as well as crabby and curmudgeonly. But I changed. I recognized that compassion was not about another person's capacity to love me but about my own power to love.

Compassion can also include setting our own boundaries to establish healthier relationships, or even the absence of ongoing relationship. For example, consider a family that grapples with the drug addiction of a family member who has stolen from them. Other members of the family might choose to forgive and have compassion for the one with the ongoing addiction, but they also draw clear lines so as not to enable the family member and to protect their own sense of well-being. They might tell him that he cannot live at home until he is sober or require that he be in ongoing structured treatment of a certain sort while he is living at home. Compassion is not the absence of boundaries but rather the understanding that healthy boundaries establish the safe space for healing and forgiveness to take place.

Love is powerful. Jesus' life shows us that love is the greatest power there is, a power that triumphs over even death. We can choose the path of compassion. When we do, we may discover that, as with Jesus, there is a power within us to love that can never be harmed by any other human being's action—not even one that crucifies.

Jesus offers us a remarkable model from the cross in how he enacts forgiveness: He remained true to his own nature, as a being who is capable of love and compassion, even when he was being crucified. *His power is in his compassion*, a power that is not only divine but also human. We are recipients of the Holy Spirit, and so we, like Jesus, are bearers of this divine compassion. On the cross, Jesus emptied himself of everything except love. Can we let go of the need to control? Can we empty ourselves of the need to know? Can we instead embrace our deepest identity, an identity that is capable of great love?

Here are some suggestions for prayer.

- What do you understand about the situation at hand, and what feels confusing and unknown? Where are the places that you feel *you* have not been fully known or understood? What would it mean for God to know and to witness your experience even if this other person does not? Bring your experience to God in prayer. Let God respond.

- Imagine Jesus on the cross, looking down at the soldiers, his mother, his friends, and strangers. What does Jesus' face look like as he forgives? How does his voice sound? How do those beneath the cross respond to his forgiveness? How do you want to respond?

- Choose a favorite familiar place and imagine being there. Perhaps it is a beach, the memory of a tree house from childhood, a beautiful place in nature, or a cozy space in your own home. Invite Jesus to come and sit in this place with you. Speak to Jesus about all your thoughts and feelings. Then wait and imagine Jesus speaking to you in reply. What does Jesus want to show you about this situation right now?

- Identify a time in the past when you experienced compassion from God or from another person. Revisit those feelings of being the recipient of compassion. Reflect on where in your life you would like to increase compassion or self-compassion.

From Death to Life

Jesus Christ, may your death be my life
and in your dying may I learn how to live.
May your struggles be my rest,
Your human weakness my courage,
Your embarrassment my honor,
Your passion my delight,
Your sadness my joy,
in your humiliation may I be exalted.
In a word, may I find all my blessings in your trials.
Amen.

—Peter Faber, SJ

Step Four

Trust in Abundant Grace

This next step on the road might well seem like a detour. Sometimes when I am using my phone's GPS on a road trip, I am surprised by the suggestions that the guidance program makes. For example, exit the highway now and take what looks like a smaller road, only to rejoin the same highway later. Yet when the trip is a longer one, sometimes what looks like the longer way on paper turns out to be faster, or at least more pleasant.

Jesus tells a parable about forgiveness that on the surface looks as though it has a simple but hard message: forgive, otherwise God will not forgive you. When we look more deeply into what Jesus is saying, however, it turns out that Jesus takes us on a bit of an apparent detour on the longer road to forgiveness. This detour, however, brings us closer to the destination, although it may not seem so until we have traveled for a while in that direction.

The parable goes like this. Once, there was a servant who owed ten thousand bags of gold to his master. While at first the servant is told to sell all he owns, and even his wife and children, to repay the debt, when he begs and pleads for more time, the master does even better. The master is merciful and forgives the debt completely. He lets the man go. Later, however, the same servant sees a fellow servant who owes him a mere one hundred coins of silver. From him, he aggressively demands repayment, even choking him. This servant also asks for patience, but instead of receiving mercy, he is thrown into jail. When others hear about it, outraged, they tell the master, who throws the ungrateful servant into jail to be punished until he has paid back his debt. Jesus briefly interprets the parable: "So my heavenly Father will also do to every one of you, if you do not forgive your brother or sister from your heart" (Matthew 18:35).

For a long time, I found this parable to be troublesome. I did not like it at all. The parable locates what is so hard about forgiveness for so many of us: our great desire to be its recipient while often struggling to be its giver. That part of it feels honest to me. But I have also thought that the parable makes forgiveness look a bit too much like an economic interchange. Am I really supposed to forgive another person only so that I can be forgiven? How is that genuine forgiveness and not just lobbying for my own status with God? The God I know from prayer is not a God of tit for tat. Moreover, one reason I want to forgive is to be free of feelings such as anger or resentment. If I forgive another only because I want forgiveness myself, this doesn't seem to help with those feelings at all! Instead, I might go through the motions of forgiving and still find myself upset, angry, or hurt the next time I see the person.

However, if we look more deeply at the story that Jesus tells, it turns out that the parable is not really about forgiving others to avoid God's wrath. The story is about something much deeper: trusting in the plenitude of God's abundant grace.

Life as a Gift

Jesus' parable is a response to Peter's question as to how many times he ought to forgive his brother: Up to seven? Jesus answers not only seven but seventy-seven—or, really, to forgive without end. The parable is designed to address the specific concern that Peter, and so many of us, might have: when is it "enough"? Peter is like a good accountant, wanting to know what he owes and what he does not. Maybe as a fisherman, Peter had to be a good accountant, determining how many fish he needed each day to make a good living, what price he ought to ask for, and how to budget his funds across the course of a year when the season for fishing likely varied. Jesus, though, asked Peter and the other fishermen to leave their nets behind when they followed him. What looks like a parable about the economics of forgiveness turns out to be more about the abundance of grace.

Let's go back to the details of the parable. In this story, Jesus asks us to enter the problem of forgiveness from multiple perspectives. We see the perspective of the merciful master, who also has a concern for justice and injustice. We see the perspective of the servant who receives mercy and fails to pass it on. We see the perspective of the person who doesn't receive mercy at all. We can even experience the point of view of the indignant bystanders.

Forgiveness is a process in which we are asked to see a situation from a view other than our own, to try to understand and to empathize with how our situation looks from different points of view. Most of us can recall times when we have been the forgiving person and times when we have been the one in need of forgiveness. Yet there is more to the parable.

Jesus focuses on the servant who receives mercy and forgiveness but does not pass it on. This, of course, is often our own situation with respect to God. God looks at our sins, shortcomings, and failures with gentleness, patience, and tremendous tenderness—not because justice does not matter to God but because God recognizes our incapacity to repay God. While we might be tempted to think that the parable is merely about an economics of forgiveness, in which we are forgiven our sins and so must forgive the sins of others, this metaphor of ten thousand bags of gold suggests that more is going on here. Ten thousand bags of gold is an enormous sum; it does not simply represent "a lot." It is not just a debt that is hard to pay back. "Ten thousand bags of gold" represents more wealth than we can ever repay.

So here is a suggestion: what if the gold that the servant "owes" his master in repayment does not represent what we owe God for our *sins* but rather what we "owe" God for all the *good gifts* that God constantly bestows on us?

Everything we have is a gift, and yet we can often act as though what we are given belongs to us, as though we have earned it by ourselves. This is how the unforgiving servant thinks about the money he lent out to others. He treats the money as though it is his own, and therefore he demands repayment. But where did he get the hundred coins of silver that he lent to his fellow servant? From among the ten thousand bags of gold that he was first given. The servant has forgotten that all he possesses did not come from himself but from the generosity of his master.

Now it becomes a little clearer how Jesus' parable is a response to Peter's question. Peter wants to count the cost of forgiveness, to place a limit and a finite quantity on what is and is not forgivable. Peter acts like an economist, trying to calculate the amount of forgiveness required to be a good person or—in Peter's case—a worthy disciple. But God's grace is like thousands of bags, each full of hundreds of coins: uncountable. All that we receive and all that we can give to others, or receive from them, first has its origin in the uncountable, abundant generosity of God. Jesus is not really interested in answering the question of what the minimum amount of forgiveness is to be "okay" in God's eyes. Jesus wants to invite Peter into something much deeper and more surprising: gratitude for the generosity of divine love, *the recognition of immeasurable grace.*

Jesus' parable gives us reasons to offer mercy and forgiveness to others, over and over again. First, we are reminded that the good we are given in love by our creator God is far beyond anything that others owe us. Others do not owe us anything. As one spiritual director phrased it, "Everything is a gift." Do we take that idea seriously? To focus on what we believe others owe us, or what we have lost on account of their actions, is to fail to see the abundance all around us. When we treat life in terms of what is owed, we lose sight of the gifts we have. *Everything* is a gift. Just as the servant forgets about the generosity of the master who has forgiven his debt when he runs into his own debtor, we, too, easily forget about God's ongoing graciousness to us.

Ignatius thought that all of our decisions ought to be grounded in a vision of life in which we recognize that all we are given is a gift and so we are free to love no matter what comes our way: whether we are rich or poor, are sick or healthy, or live a long life or a short one. To that end, he proposed the First Principle and Foundation of the Spiritual Exercises. According to Ignatius, we are to see all that God gives us as a gift that we are to use, as good stewards, in freedom. Freedom here means a freedom to use our gifts in a way that promotes love and to live out our missions. Some good gifts have to be let go or set aside for us to continue along our way. We also must be willing to receive new gifts in freedom, even while acknowledging that someday we will have to let go of these. Life involves change and loss; it also includes continually new gifts from God. Yet we easily focus on the few coins of silver we have lost instead of the thousands of bags of gold that God offers.

Why do we so often fail to see everything and everyone we are given as gifts? Why do we so easily mistreat others as though their love, loyalty, and usefulness are somehow owed to us? I believe this failure of sight is our way of avoiding the vulnerability of love: Whether we are falling in love with a person, a community of people, a job, or a way of life, love makes us vulnerable. It is scary to fall in love and even scarier when I recognize that another person is not mine but God's. Even the most faithful spouse is not mine forever, because it is possible that he might die before I do. My sweet toddler will grow up to have an independent life. My best friend could move away. A job that provides a sense of meaning and fulfillment, or the respect of a colleague, might be temporary. I am less vulnerable when I believe that the job is mine because I have worked for it than when I believe it is a gift from God. When we can let go of what we believe we are owed and focus instead on ourselves as recipients of unearned gifts, we become freer to forgive. Relationships stop being about what we are owed. Rather, they become interactions freely offered and freely given. This frees us to forgive.

In this way, this parable about forgiveness is related to Jesus' sermons in which he counsels us not to worry about the person who takes our cloak but to give him our tunic as well (Matthew 5:40; Luke 6:29), or the lilies of the field, which do not worry about clothing (Matthew 6:28; Luke 12:27). The servant who is forgiven his sins not only fails to recall that he has been forgiven for his debt but also fails to recognize that what others owe him never really belonged to him in the first place but was always a gift from above.

Some of our struggles with forgiveness can be over what we think another person owes us. In some ways this is natural: we seek justice, and justice can include the restoration of what is owed or off balance. Consider the earlier example of Jeff and Julie, and Julie's wish that her brother Jeff had done more while their mother was ill and she was carrying a lot of the work of caregiving. Julie could not really go back in time and get what she wanted from Jeff during their mother's illness. But she was able to let go of some of her resentment toward Jeff when she reframed how she thought about her brother. One day when he was in a minor car accident, she began to reflect on what a gift her brother's life was to her. Perhaps she might have been an only child, with no brother at all to lean on during her mother's illness. She began to reflect on the graciousness of many acts of love that Jeff often showed her, from the way he joked around with her to cheer her up when she was feeling down to the long phone calls between them during their mother's illness. Julie started to see her brother's presence in her life as a gift, even if he was not always perfect. By reflecting on how her brother was a gift from God to her, she began to let go of the past.

Jesus' parable reminds us of something essential in the process of forgiveness: *God offers a kind of wholesome, healing, abundant love that no other person ever can.* Ten thousand bags of gold cannot capture the enormity of God's riches of love. Do I live out of that knowledge of God's abundance in my dealings with others, or do I reduce who and what others are to what I think they should be to and for me? In this parable, it is not the master, or God, who acts like an accountant but rather *we* who count out every coin. God, however, forgives our debts anyway and then asks us to do the same for others—because God is the origin of all gifts in the first place.

The Pearl of Great Price

I have found that I can do this inner work of forgiveness only when I know how deeply beloved I am by God. I remember one prayer during which I experienced this profoundly. I decided to pray with the image of Jesus as the pearl of great price. In my imagination, I was standing on a beach, digging into the sand to find this pearl. I stood on the beach, digging with a long shovel, deeper and deeper into the ground. At one point, my shovel struck a clay jar, which I understood to symbolize an earthen vessel or symbol of my flawed yet gifted nature. Yet this still was not the pearl. I dug even further until I could not see down the hole, and my shovel would go no further. I had run out of my own resources. So, in my prayer, I jumped into the depths of the darkness. As I imagined looking down at myself from above, I suddenly saw that there was a pearl inside me, glowing inside my own throat, within my own body deep in the darkness. I understood that Christ was not only in other people who had embodied God's love for me but also in myself, in my own capacity to love. Beneath all my false, egoistic, sometimes narcissistic layers that sought love from others, I, too, held this treasure within.

This is true for every human being. Jesus is the pearl of great price, but in God's eyes, each of us is also that treasured pearl. Only when I know my own worth am I free to forgive from a real and authentic place. The unforgiving servant does not recognize the plenitude of God's love, and he does not recognize that he himself is capable of acting like God, as one who sets others free from their debts. This is not just a problem of failing to act ethically. It is about recognizing and honoring one's deepest and most authentic self. We, too, are invited by God to honor our true selves, the people we are at the core of our being: capable of love of self, love of others, and forgiveness of debts, all grounded in the knowledge that we are loved by God.

Jesus ends the parable with the recommendation that we forgive "from the heart." What are some practical ways to do so?

- Identify with honesty whether you feel that you are owed something. If so, what are the real desires and longings of your heart that are not currently being met? Name these for God, and simply present them to God in prayer. Can you imagine God meeting these needs out of God's abundant love? Are there other places in your life that God is generously offering to meet these desires?

- In Jesus' parable, the master listens to his servant, but then the servant does not pass on this grace and listen to his fellow servant. Are you being invited into better listening in this situation? Is a conversation called for in which you can listen more deeply to the other person's perspective?

- Set aside the question of forgiveness of the other person for a while. Instead, simply focus on where God is abundantly gifting you with blessings. What are the gifts of the past day? the past month? the past year?

Spend time soaking in memories and experiences of the abundance that God continually offers you.

- What is in your "treasure box"? Where in your life have you loved and been loved? How might God treasure this aspect of you: your own capacity to love?

Principle and Foundation

God who loves us, creates us and wants to share life with us forever. Our love response takes shape in our praise and honor and service of the God of our life.

All the things in this world are also created because of God's love, and they become a context of gifts, presented to us so that we can know God more easily and make a return of love more readily.

As a result, we show reverence for all the gifts of creation and collaborate with God in using them so that by being good stewards, we develop as loving persons in our care of God's world and its development. But if we abuse any of these gifts of creation or, on the contrary, take them as the center of our lives, we break our relationship with God and hinder our growth as loving persons.

In everyday life, then, we must hold ourselves in balance before all created gifts insofar as we have a choice and are not bound by some responsibility. We should not fix our desires on health or sickness, wealth or poverty, success or failure, a long life or a short one. For everything has the potential of calling forth in us a more loving response to our life forever with God.

Our only desire and our one choice should be this: I want and I choose what better leads to God's deepening life in me.[6]

—From the *Spiritual Exercises* by Ignatius Loyola, adapted by David Fleming, SJ

Step Five

Leave behind the Locked Room (Forgive Yourself)

A friend once described his life's journey as a series of stops and starts. Sometimes, he said, he feels as though he has to put down his backpack and rest awhile. He sits and stubbornly refuses to move forward, even when he knows he should. Eventually, however, something changes: a word of encouragement, the shift of an internal season, or enough rest so that he has the energy to move forward again. In considering his metaphor, I thought of a time when Jesus' disciples also get stuck. After the Passion, the disciples go into a locked room and are afraid to come out. In my own processes of forgiving others, sometimes I have become so self-protective that I have ended up in something like a locked room, an interior space where I refuse to move forward in life. I have become stubborn or trapped inside my own fears or the stories inside my head.

Sometimes, in a situation where we struggle to forgive others, we need to let God forgive us for our part in the situation. God always offers us forgiveness. For us as Christians, every time we look at the cross, we are invited to look at a love that saves and redeems, that is willing to go all the way to death and beyond to invite us into forgiveness and life beyond it. For me, the sacrament of reconciliation allows not only for God to forgive me but also for me to experience that reconciling love in an embodied way.

We also need to practice self-forgiveness. Allowing God to forgive me does not mean that I have forgiven myself. Ignatius himself struggled with scrupulosity, a desire to go to confession repeatedly and to be overly focused on his own sins. What is going on when I find it hard to forgive myself even though I know that God loves and forgives me?

One way to think about it is to understand that we are divided inside. The "I" that I am now may look back at the "me" that I was at the time I acted sinfully and find it hard to reconcile these two into one person. And yet both are who I am. Unless the "I" that judges myself can be aligned with the God who loves and forgives, who sees with compassion and understanding the "me" who acted sinfully, then I will remain trapped. I must not only allow God to free me but also be willing to follow God into a vision of myself as God sees me. Again, this is the work of the imagination, of how I can re-envision myself.

After the Passion is over, in one of the Resurrection scenes, Jesus comes to the disciples, who are locked away in a hidden room. For them, both these elements were present: fear about what harm might come to them from others if they left the room and guilt over how they had abandoned and betrayed Jesus. I find it helpful to remember this: The very people Jesus chose to be his companions are the same ones who abandoned Jesus, fled in fear from him, and became stuck on the road of their mission as apostles. Yet the story does not end there for them, and neither does it for us.

Let's imagine the scene for a moment from the point of view of being a disciple:

Imagine that you are sitting in a locked room, behind a closed door: heavy, wooden, latched securely. At least you hope so. You are with your friends, people you have known for years now. Unfortunately, a close friend in the group was killed recently. At the time, you knew there might be danger. The political situation in the area was more tumultuous than many people realized. Your friend was outspoken, rarely afraid of the authorities—even when you reminded him that he might do more good by being a little quieter and more careful about it. He was both humble and yet somehow confident that God would take care of it all, always reassuring you that God was at work, even in the most adverse circumstances. He was so loving and centered that you believed it. He prayed often and rarely worried. At least until that one night when they finally came to take him away; then his sweat and tears were more than you could stand to see. You'd said that you would be loyal, even be willing to die for him, but like most of the others, you fell asleep rather than sit up with him. Then, when the danger came, you ran away altogether.

Now, inside this locked room, you wait in fear, seated on a mat on the floor. A friend walks over with a piece of bread to eat, and you remind him not to let his shoes make too much sound on the hard floor, in case someone can hear. He takes off his shoes, and you remember the day when your friend also took off your shoes, tenderly washed your feet, and reminded you to love one another. How far away those days feel. This morning looks nothing like life did only a week ago, and it is not clear when it is going to get any better. You shut your eyes and try to imagine birds, lilies, a lush open field, the kinds of things that he would want us to remember as symbols of trust.

Suddenly, there is a crashing sound: someone has dropped a cup, startled. The cup breaks, and water spills all over the floor. Another man standing near the door gasps. Jesus is here, standing in your midst. And yet the door is still closed, the latch locked tightly as ever. He walks over to each person in the room, embraces him, and leans over, whispering something into the person's ear. You strain to hear what it is, but the sound escapes you. What could it be? Your anxiety is ratcheted up, and a small knot forms in your throat. Finally, Jesus approaches you, too: his warm, brown eyes meet yours, and you see a gentle radiance on his face. He places his arms around you, just as he used to, looks you in the eye as he stands before you, and then leans in. "Peace be with you. Your sins are forgiven. Now, go out and forgive." You feel his breath on your cheek as he speaks, and along with it, a feeling of peace and warmth, a kind of groundedness. As he stands back, your joy meets his, and something inside you is alive again—something new that has never grown there before in quite this way. Not much later, Jesus leaves, but although he is absent in the flesh, you feel in your heart that he will never leave you and that this time he is here to stay.

When Jesus comes to his friends locked away in the upper room, he does more than forgive them for where they fell short. He also missions them to go out and forgive others. Choosing to forgive is not only about letting go of anger, fear, or resentment so that I can be free to go and live out my own life. Choosing to forgive is also part of God's mission for the world: a mission to heal, to redeem, and to bring others back to life so that they are no longer locked up but are set free. How surprising it must have been for the disciples in the room to hear not only that they were forgiven but also that Jesus had a job for them to do: to go out and do the work of forgiveness with others.

Incarnation and Mission

In the second week of the Spiritual Exercises, Ignatius asks us to imagine the Trinity looking down on the earth in all its sinfulness and deciding to enter that world for its redemption. He encourages us to spend time considering what is going through God's heart and mind as he chooses to enter this world and all its chaos, to imagine what God feels and thinks in making this merciful decision. I recall praying with this on one occasion, when I heard God say, "I sent you, too." Of course, God did not mean that I was God incarnate! None of us is God in power or wisdom. But we do share in the call to enter a broken world. We know from Pentecost and from our own reception of the Holy Spirit at our baptism and confirmation that we, too, are sent to heal the world. We are not to remain locked up in our room, any more than God stayed away from the human world, locked up in heaven. God came into the human world, a world of messiness and difficulty.

Ignatian spirituality has sometimes described Satan or the "evil spirit" as the "enemy of human nature." The meaning of this phrase became clear to me only when my colleague Michael Himes at Boston College explained it this way: Satan has no problem with God being God. Satan thinks God is fine because God is perfect. What Satan objects to is that human beings are not God, that they are less than perfect. Satan's objection to the human being is precisely that we are not good enough. And it is this belief in the human person in all its frailty being not good enough that leads people into despair.[7]

Hope is not grounded in the belief that someday human beings will become gods but rather the idea that God already loves human beings as we are and that it is from this being loved *as is* that we find the courage to accept the grace to grow in love and so also to grow in sanctity, without becoming sanctimonious.

In Scripture, Jesus calls Peter and James, who are fishermen (Matthew 4:18–20). When they got up to follow him, they "left their nets." We, too, have our nets that we must put down if we are to take up the call to follow Jesus. Nets can catch fish, but they can also entangle and hold us back from what God is asking us to do. It helps for us to take a look at what the nets are that hold us back from forgiving. If we have a clear sense of a call to forgive, we might find it easy to follow God, but we might also have to put down our nets first. These nets can be expectations of other people; a sense of pride; an excessive desire for self-protection; or being enslaved to old "scripts" that come from still-older relationships. When we let go of these nets, we are freer to follow Jesus into new places and to partake in God's mission. Forgiveness itself is part of that divine missioning. We are not called to forgive others simply so that we can go on and do the work God gives us to do. *Forgiveness is itself part of God's redeeming work.*

But we have to make a fundamental choice, one that God does not force us to make. We are invited to make this choice, but it requires our consent, and we can say no. The choice is this: Do we want to take up God's mission to love people as human beings and to love ourselves this way, too? Do we want to take up the mission to leave behind the locked room of fear and self-righteousness and go out into a world to minister to others as they really are, recognizing that to be a human being is to be lovable, even with all our faults and failings?[8]

A person I know, "Jenny," shares the story of how she struggled with self-forgiveness after a suicide threat. This threat against her own life was brought on by struggles with PTSD coupled with the end of an important relationship. Jenny explained to me that while she had gone to the sacrament of reconciliation and expressed genuine contrition over what she had threatened to do, she also struggled to forgive herself. Jenny knew that God loved and forgave her. Yet she continued to regret her actions and to feel caught up in their power. The question and decision for her was, could she also love herself? Jenny shared that eventually she felt able to forgive herself when she re-envisioned herself not only as a victim but also as a person who had purpose in life, given to her by God. Through psychotherapy she was able to pursue healing for her PTSD, but an equally important part of her healing was to recognize that she had a mission in life. She was not reducible to her suicide threat or her struggles with mental illness. Jenny was created by God to love and to offer her gifts and talents to the larger world.

All of us have a mission—not only priests or religious who may name their life's vocation in terms of mission but also every Christian person, whether lay or religious. God calls us to love and to be ministers of healing and love. How we enact that love and healing of the world's brokenness is different for each one of us, but every person has a purpose that embodies love in some way. To enact that mission of love, however, we must come out of the locked room and leave behind the fears that trap us inside it.

A line from Scripture that I once came across on a paper bookmark was especially helpful to me in thinking about my own struggles with self-forgiveness. The bookmark quoted St. Paul: "My grace is sufficient for you, for power is made perfect in weakness" (2 Corinthians 12:9). On the bookmark were black and white outlines of a growing plant with a flower on top, waiting to be colored in. I wondered, why the flowers? How does a flower blossom out of weakness? As a gardener, though, I considered all the ways that flowers really do arise from ground that is not perfect. For example, in one area of my yard, I have to add compost to the soil and break it up with a hoe every year to aerate the soil. My compost comes from all my kitchen leftovers, the garbage after I prepare a meal. There are even traces of old eggshells and the occasional avocado pit that inadvertently makes its way into the compost. St. Paul recognized something truthful about our weaknesses: God uses even our weaknesses and limits for the greater good, like the bad garbage that gets turned into good compost. I can think of many students who have served in the service learning program at my college over the years.

Some of the most gifted students are those who have struggled in some way themselves: for example, the student who has confronted and dealt with his own dependency on alcohol may prove to be an especially compassionate volunteer when working with a homeless person with an addiction. By ourselves, our weaknesses can undo us, but when offered to God, they can be turned into something beautiful. We can color in the outlines of the plant that God has traced out for us. We can grow beautiful flowers from experience's rich soil.

What does your "locked room" look like? What does it take for you to come out and journey forward again? What would it mean to offer this same sort of freedom to the person you are seeking to forgive?

Here are some suggestions for prayer.

1. Imagine the Trinity looking down at our world and its birth and death, illness, crime, poverty, acts of injustice, gossip, and despair (see St. Ignatius's "Contemplation of the Incarnation"). How does God feel as God looks down at this world and decides to enter it and become incarnate in the person of Jesus? What might be going through God's mind and heart? Can you identify at all with God's desire to love a broken and sinful world?

2. Do the imaginative prayer in number 1 again, on a separate occasion, but this time imagine that God is asking

you to become a human being, to walk the road that is your life's path, in order to undertake a mission of love. What is God asking you to do in joining this world with all its human imperfections? How do you want to respond to God?

3. Imagine being inside a locked room as one of the disciples. When Jesus embraces you, he asks you to pass on forgiveness to others. What do you need to hear before you open the door, rejoin the world, and enact the work of forgiveness? Ask God for what you need.

4. Pray with the imagery of the fishermen putting down their nets: what nets do you need to put down to follow Jesus' call? One way to pray with the imagery of the nets is to imagine what the nets stand for in a symbolic way. For example, am I trapped by resentment? I might imagine the net as smoldering and set it aside into the sea as I follow Jesus. Am I trapped by an inability to forgive myself? I might imagine Jesus lifting the net off me and pulling me to my feet so I can go on my way. Feel free to play with the imagery.

Examen of God's Compassion and Mercy for Me

1. I begin by giving thanks for the good gifts God has given me so far.

2. I ask God for the gifts of insight and illumination into my own situation as a loved sinner.

3. I review my past, allowing whatever comes to mind to arise, considering times when God was merciful, kind, and compassionate with me in my own limits and sin.

4. I consider where I have allowed that mercy to sink in and inform how I act with others and where I have not yet fully integrated that love into my own actions.

5. I ask God for any insight or assistance in guiding a response to what I have experienced in prayer today.

Step Six

Let Go and Make Friends with Time

Years before he founded the Society of Jesus, Ignatius went on a pilgrimage to the Holy Land. He had already been on a journey of transformation, leaving behind the life of a nobleman and soldier to become a poor soldier for Christ. Yet he had clear ideas about what he thought his life might look like that were entirely different from how his life turned out. Ignatius set out for the Holy Land, where he hoped to devote his life to God. Despite no money and advice that such a trip could not be made without money, he succeeded in traveling there. However, once he arrived in Jerusalem, Ignatius was turned away and told to go back home by Franciscans who said they could not assure him of his safety. Ignatius did not really want to leave but finally listened to what the

Franciscan provincial told him to do. Imagine if Ignatius had never returned to Spain, then gone on to Rome—the Society of Jesus might never have been founded! Yet at the time, he must have wondered greatly about the meaning of such a long trip if he was only to be sent back home.

One of the hardest truths about forgiveness is that the future after forgiveness often does not look much like anyone's ideas about it. We might, for example, imagine that once forgiveness and reconciliation arrive, we will go back to some past time—perhaps real only in our fantasies. Alternatively, we may try to determine what the future looks like by placing restrictions on what forgiveness might look like or on what shape or form healing must have. Sometimes we have to let go of the past and let go of the future if we are to see where God is leading us in the present moment.

While Ignatian spirituality affirms the use of the imagination, we also must be able to distinguish imagination from mere fantasy. To do this, we have to look closely at the way the world is today, rather than in the past. Sometimes when we go on a road trip as a family, my husband will read aloud a book to the family while I drive, or the kids will play video games in the backseat. By the time they look up and out the window again, the scenery has changed substantially. On the journey of forgiveness, we may find that the landscape of our relationship or our community has changed substantially since the last time we looked.

One way I have sometimes thought about this is akin to the ghosts from Charles Dickens's *A Christmas Carol.* There is the ghost of the past, the ghost of the future, and the ghost of the present. The ghost of the past is my name for the past that I imagine but that never was: either an ideal relationship that was always perfect before a break or a person or relationship that was always evil, for example. Maybe I imagine that my spouse and I will relate as we did when we first began to date one another—when both of us were too new to our relationship to truly see ourselves or one another as we really were. Or I might remember that my colleague was "always" unkind and "never" treated me with gentleness or good disposition. But this kind of black-and-white thinking is likely to be more about my own fantasy than the reality of human beings.

Likewise, the "ghost of the future" can be a way of naming a fantastic idea of what a healed or reconciled relationship would look like. For example, I might imagine that healing a rift with my political enemy will take place when he finally converts to my way of thinking about the world. Or I may think that a romantic relationship or marriage can be resumed only if my partner relates to me in the same ways he did in our honeymoon phase, even though we have both out-grown this way of relating. Until I let go of the fantasy that I will make another person into my own image of whom I wish for him to be, there is an obstacle to forgiveness.

The "ghost of the present" is perhaps the most deceptive of all the ghosts to claim and to name, because self-deception and fantasies about the present are the hardest to identify. For example, a friend of mine once spoke longingly of her hope that her former fiancé would regret breaking off the engage-ment and might in fact be secretly missing her but was too shy to say so. All of us around her understood that her desires were not in line with reality. He had simply moved on, and it was her own constructions of a reality that did not exist that prevented her from moving forward. Only when she faced facts and did the work of grieving her former fiancé was she able to forgive and begin to consider other relational possi-bilities. In attempting to understand what our own "ghosts of the present" might be, we can talk to others whom we trust and who know our situation well. Ignatian spirituality often recommends that we discuss our discernment with oth-ers so that they can provide feedback about what is realistic and what is not.

Forgiveness is all about letting go: letting go of the past, letting go of an imagined future, and living more fully in the present, a present that is real but beautiful in its realness. Vinita Hampton Wright identifies four reasons we can resist letting go: We can resist because "letting go feels like a failure." We can resist because we have not found a new habit or new alternative to our old attachment. We can resist because we are comfortable with an old emotional pattern—even ones that we tell ourselves we do not want! Or, as she writes, "I resist letting go because I don't want to face my root problems."[9]

Making Friends with Time

For me, learning to live in the present has also meant making friends with time. Part of me can still sometimes resist the very notion that the past is not subject to being relived and "done over" again, only this time without mistakes. When we watch a sports event, like a game of football, and watch how a mistake in a play occurred, we can rewind the tape and look at the tape to see what went wrong. Part of us might also wish that we could literally go back in time and stop the event from ever having happened. We don't want to fumble the ball or kick it sideways. We wish that the penalty play had never taken place, because the outcome of the entire game changed as a result. Wouldn't it be good if we could do it all over again? But while God gives us the gift of forgiveness, this does not come in the form of an infinite number of do-overs. Sometimes our spouses, friends, parents, and children do give us a real chance to try again, this time in the right way. When this happens, it is a great blessing. But we cannot always keep pushing the rewind button and trying again. For this we should be thankful; otherwise, life might never move forward at all!

Instead, in our forgiving we must embrace the reality of time that does move forward while we recognize that some events are not capable of being undone but must be integrated into the present. This does not mean that something new cannot be created in their place. Neither does it mean that the love and care we experienced in the past are lost forever. I once had a prayer experience in which I was saying goodbye to a person who was very beloved to me. Jesus handed me a pocket watch on which there were no hands. In my prayer, Jesus said to me, "The amount of time doesn't matter." What Jesus meant by that, I understood, was that the amount of time we love a person does not matter in terms of the love that remains with us. We might love a parent or grandparent who dies, for example, or a friend who moves away. We might have experienced love with a person with whom we can no longer remain in active, day-to-day relationship and conversation. But the love between us remains. Like a clock that does not need hands to tell time, love itself is eternal and not bound by space, time, or even physical proximity.

What does all this have to do with forgiveness? I have found it easier to forgive when I realize that time is also a gift. *Time is a means by which I can grow in love and forgiveness.* God gives me time to forgive. God's love crisscrosses time; love is not linear in the way that normal time is. For example, whenever we return to God in prayer and hold in our hearts the memory of a person we have lost, that love is still there. Love remains present at the Eucharist when we pray for those who have loved us and departed us, even if forgiveness takes place long after death. Love remains present when we pray for those who are still alive, still making their earthly pilgrimage, even if we are not in active relationship now and not likely to be so until we are back home again, together in the wider community of saints. Love remains when we let go, because God keeps that love for us inside God's own heart, a heart in which we also reside.

Touching Jesus' Healed Wounds

The story about the encounter between Jesus and Thomas can also teach us something about how to make friends with time—and how to make friends with our healed wounds, too. When Jesus appears to the disciples in the locked room, Thomas is absent. Although his friends tell him what they have experienced, Thomas wants proof. Interestingly,

Thomas asks not for proof of life but proof of Jesus' wounds. For Thomas, the question is not only whether there is a Jesus who is alive and raised from the dead; perhaps there is also a doubt on Thomas's part as to whether Jesus really was raised. But I would suggest an even deeper question in Thomas's demand to see Jesus' wounds. Thomas wishes to know, *Is this Jesus that they have seen raised from the dead the same Jesus who suffered and was wounded? Is there a real continuity between his human life—his sorrow, suffering, and death—and this raised Jesus?* Thomas wants to know it, and literally to touch it: "Unless I see the mark of the nails in his hands and put my finger in the mark of the nails and my hand in his side, I will not believe" (John 20:25).

Thomas's demand that his own hands enter Jesus' wounds is also an entry point for us, to help us to make sense of our own suffering. Perhaps one of the most frustrating responses we are offered when we're in pain—whether physical, emotional, or spiritual—is another's well-meaning attempt to placate pain by suggesting that the suffering will end. Of course, in many cases this is true: for example, spraining one's ankle in a competition is often a temporary pain and inconvenience. But in many of the deepest experiences of suffering, we know that suffering will not be followed by a return to stasis. Unlike television sitcoms, where each challenge is resolved by the episode's end and we witness a return to the same old situation, real lives undergo fundamental alterations. Often the challenge is to learn how to incorporate pain into one's ongoing experience.

Parents who suffer the intense grief of losing a child often report that life never returns to normal but that they must learn to incorporate the grief and pain in a way that life can still meaningfully move forward. Women who are traumatized by rape or soldiers traumatized by war may experience their own "resurrections," but such resurrection is not a return to what was before. Even smaller but significant losses, such as losing a job, a promising athletic career to an injury, or a valued relationship, can have enduring effects. In some cases of forgiveness, the goal may not be to eliminate the wounds. It may be the case that forgiveness helps us live with *transformed wounds* instead. John's Gospel opens the possibility of understanding resurrection as a transformation in which wounds are healed but remain as openings.

When Jesus appears to Thomas, the Gospel is careful to point out that this is a week later (John 20:26). Whatever Jesus' resurrected body looks like—that it is transformed is clear in John's Gospel—it permanently carries with it the marks of suffering. Jesus' body remains marked with his wounds even after the Resurrection. In this Resurrection encounter, Jesus invites Thomas to enter his wounds: "Put your finger here and see my hands. Reach out your hand and put it in my side. Do not doubt but believe" (John 20:27). Although Thomas and the others have seen the risen Lord, they still desire to enter more deeply into this encounter, into a moment of touch. Why does John draw our attention to these marks and Jesus' invitation to touch them? I suggest that it is because his wounds provide an opening through which we, his disciples, can enter a new life ourselves. His hands are like our hands. We can know others in their suffering and be with them because we, too, have suffered and because our greatest Friend knows and shares our wounds with us. The Resurrection has not meant the undoing of history but rather its transformation.

Transformed Wounds and Service

In my experience of forgiving those who have hurt me, I have learned that wounds sometimes stay with me, but in a transformed way, just like Jesus' healed wounds. But the scars are no longer simply reminders of a past pain. Transformed and healed wounds can become a kind of opening into compassionate relationship with others, if we let them. In an essay on service, Rachel Remen says, "When we serve, we don't serve with our strength; we serve with ourselves, and we draw from all of our experiences. Our limitations serve; our wounds serve; even our darkness can serve. My pain is the source of my compassion; my woundedness is the key to my empathy."[10] Jesus' wounds do more than give us faith in the Resurrection. We can model Jesus and his willingness to allow his wounds to be touched in a way that helps us develop our relationships with others and bring healing to them as well.

For example, when I visit men who are incarcerated, I can draw upon my past experiences of feeling abandoned or lonely in listening with care to their concerns. When they speak of their mistakes and sins, I can recall situations in which I have been sinful or acted out of my own brokenness in my relationships with others. I may not share the details of these experiences, but in a general way I do try to bring to the conversation what I have learned and what I understand as our human struggles. I can better understand why God chose to have Jesus carry his transformed wounds on his body, because I no longer think about my wounds as markers of events that I wish had never happened. Instead, I can think of my healed wounds as resources and gifts and as marks of a human history that includes sorrow as well as joy.

One day, a man named Michael sitting next to me in a prison group drew a picture of a hand dipped into a pool of water, creating ripples. This hand had the marks of wounds on it. He asked me if I wanted to know what he had drawn. I said yes. Michael said that he drew my hand, which, like Christ's hand, was wounded, and yet my teaching and talking with the community in the prison had a beneficial ripple effect. I was moved by this beautiful recognition of how being authentically in community with others can heal others as well as promote our own healing. Healed wounds have a ripple effect in healing the wounds of others.

Sometimes when we are trying to forgive, it can even help to stop trying. We can just take a break. This became vividly clear to me one time when I was praying imaginatively with Jesus. After many years of praying Gospel scenes that took place on or near a boat, I developed the habit of sometimes praying by simply showing up in my imagination to a boat where Jesus was present and conversing with him about whatever was on my mind. One time when I was especially frustrated about a relationship in need of healing, I sat with Jesus on a boat and asked him, "What do I do? I continue to feel hurt, and I don't know how to move forward. I love this other person, yet nothing I do seems to work." Jesus replied, "Let me row," and took up the oars of the boat while I just sat as the boat moved along. Jesus was telling me to let go of trying to control the process of reconciliation and give God a chance to do some work. Indeed, God did bring this relationship to greater healing—but only when I put down the oars to let him row.

God and the Persistent Widow

In this case, a particular broken relationship was healed for me at an unexpected time and place; a number of elements fell into place, as though a broken puzzle were being restored to completeness again—but someone else was putting together the pieces. What was most surprising was that the relationship reconciled precisely when I had let go and decided that my happiness really did not depend on restoration. I had come to terms with my own powerlessness in the situation and handed it over to God. God acted where I could not.

When I brought this story to a spiritual director on my retreat, he compared my situation to the story of the persistent widow in Luke 18:2–6:

> In a certain city there was a judge who neither feared God nor had respect for people. In that city there was a widow who kept coming to him and saying, "Grant me justice against my opponent." For a while he refused; but later he said to himself, "Though I have no fear of God and no respect for anyone, yet because this widow keeps bothering me, I will grant her justice so that she may not wear me out by continually coming."

"Yes!" I said excitedly. "I am like the persistent widow!" It was my persistence in seeking reconciliation that finally made it happen.

But my director gently corrected me: "No, I meant *God* is like the widow." I laughed and realized, of course! *God* is the persistent widow who ceaselessly advocates for us. In many situations of reconciliation, we are powerless. I was powerless too. But we are not without God, who is powerfully loving and constantly creating something new out of our current condition, no matter how many mistakes we may have made. For me, as wonderful as the gift of reconciliation was, the even deeper lesson was that God is a trustworthy advocate and "persistent widow" for me, even when I do not see what is happening.

While this parable is about persistence in our own prayer, it is also about trusting that our prayer is worthwhile, in part because God is acting in ways we do not always see. Letting go and leaning into our powerlessness is not a mechanism by which we finally get what we desire. Rather, letting go and letting God act when our own actions fail us is an *act of surrender to Love*. It is an act of trust in the goodness of God and in God's desire to bring all of us back to a place of healing and wholeness—whether through God's granting our desire the way that we most hope or in some other surprising way.

We cannot undo the past, and we cannot control the future. However, I know that I can, with God's grace, live more fully into the present when I become friends with time and friends with every bit of my very human history.

Here are some prayer suggestions for making friends with time.

- What are the ghosts of the past, present, and future for you as you reflect on the relationship in need of forgiveness or reconciliation? What words or names might be good names for these ghosts? What fantasies about the past, present, or future accompany them?

- If you are still in a relationship with the person you hope to forgive, and reconciliation is a real possibility, how might letting go of a way of relating in the past open a new way for God to create relationship in the future?

- Sometimes we have a road map for relationships that can take us off course because the road ahead does not look much like the one before. Perhaps we were traveling in mountainous regions and now we are on flat land but the weather has changed. What would it mean to throw away our old maps and go forward only one step at a time? What is God's next step for you?

- Where are the places where you can surrender control and let God row for a while?

Patient Trust

Above all, trust in the slow work of God.
We are quite naturally impatient in everything
    to reach the end without delay.
We should like to skip the intermediate stages.
We are impatient of being on the way to something
    unknown, something new.
And yet it is the law of all progress
    that it is made by passing through
    some stages of instability—
    and that it may take a very long time.
And so I think it is with you;
    your ideas mature gradually—let them grow,
    let them shape themselves, without undue haste.
Don't try to force them on,
    as though you could be today what time
    (that is to say, grace and circumstances
    acting on your own good will)
    will make of you tomorrow.
Only God could say what this new spirit
    gradually forming within you will be.
Give Our Lord the benefit of believing
    that his hand is leading you,
and accept the anxiety of feeling yourself
    in suspense and incomplete.

—Pierre Teilhard de Chardin, SJ

Step Seven

Create New Narratives

My colleague Richard Kearney at Boston College has undertaken the work of political reconciliation through the Guestbook Project.[11] The Guestbook Project involves bringing together two or more individuals from different sides of a long-entrenched political conflict—for example, Israelis and Palestinians, or Protestants and Catholics in Ireland. Each side begins with one person telling his or her own story about what the history or conflict means to him or her. The other person listens, and then the two switch places, trading the roles of speaker and listener. Both sides are invited to listen closely and to be open to the experience of the other, who may previously have been considered the stranger, the other, or even the enemy. The two people are then asked to create a shared story or narrative together. Through finding a new way to tell the story that includes both parties, they are brought closer in a process of reconciliation.

In one video that followed such a process, four teenage students in Londonderry came together to talk about the "walled city" divided by Catholic and Protestant lines, Irish and British identities. Two of the high school girls, one Protestant and the other Catholic, did something relatively simple: they exchanged school uniforms. Wearing the other's uniform, they walked together down the streets of the city, taking on the labels of the other. One expressed how much she disliked having the eyes of others upon her, as she felt looks that she thought judged her in this uniform and did not see deeper, to her true identity. This experience of "walking in the shoes" of another and wearing her clothes gave her some insight into how this other young woman experienced life in the same city. Later, the two combined their uniforms and created a kind of shared identity, bringing together Catholic and Protestant identities, which normally were so rigidly separate. A video presentation created by these students to commemorate their experience ends with a view of a former military base that has been turned into an amusement park. This image struck me as a beautiful image for forgiveness: demolishing the weaponry of fear and anger that leads to division and creating a shared space that looks not like a battlefield but rather like a playground.

Finding the way forward to a new narrative about another person after conflict can help us to forgive and heal. For example, I have a friend "Emma" who struggled to forgive her mother for past failures. The mother had struggled with substance abuse and so was often an absentee mom. Emma shares that although her mother put food on the table and was able to hold down a steady job, she was never really there emotionally for Emma growing up. As Emma herself became a mother, she meticulously avoided drinking and drug use, even refusing to use Tylenol when she had a headache so that she would not be like her own mother. When her own daughter became a young adult, however, their relationship became fractured when Emma's daughter felt too engulfed in her mother's care. Instead of being an absentee mom, Emma had difficulty allowing her adult daughter to have her own life and family without too much intervention. I remember when Emma shared with me that for the first time, she was able to really forgive her own mother for her shortcomings: "Only when my own daughter screamed at me on the phone and said, '*Get out of my life!*' and I was feeling sorry for myself about how hard it is to be a good mom, did I realize that the exact same thing had been true for my own mother too. My mother had the added burden of being a single mom under financial duress and was doing the best she could under pressure." Emma found that she could be gentler and kinder in her interactions with her mom as she developed a new narrative of her mother's actions and greater compassion for them.

Sometimes, after a conflict, we can rewrite the narrative in participation with the party with whom we have had a difficulty. If we can find a shared narrative, we may move closer toward reconciliation. It takes time to find a shared narrative, and it requires that we risk being vulnerable with one another. We need to have a degree of safety to want to embark on this journey together at all. We must be willing to put aside the weaponry of judgment, even though judgment of others can help us feel safer. We benefit from putting listening ahead of speaking. We may even have to swallow our pride and put the relationship ahead of our desire to preserve our own way of seeing or doing things. Like the teenagers in Londonderry, we have to find creative ways to turn a battlefield into a playground.

Even if the other person is not willing or able to converse, it is still possible to take on the work of retelling the narrative *with God*. Ignatian imaginative prayer can assist us in doing this kind of compassionate retelling of our own stories. Jesus' healing of the blind man Bartimaeus, for example, is a simple story that can help us pray over our own "blind spots" (Mark 10:46–52). When we spend time considering where our blind spots might be, we are more able to let go of old narratives and create new ones. For example, you might take this image of the blind person who needs to see and pray simply, "God, what do you want me to see?" Then wait to see what Jesus does or says.

A friend recently told me about a breakup with a man she had been in love with many years ago. The relationship came to an end because he simply did not love her the way she loved him. She said to me, "It took months for me to realize that part of what I had been missing was not the person himself but a whole picture of what I thought my life would look like. I had imagined myself married to this man, working at a small midwestern liberal arts college, owning a home, and having two small children. It was only after I started to envision the possibility of what else my life could look like, working and living somewhere else, that I was able to let go." Today she is married, without children but working at a job that she loves and where she contributes her many talents to a community that greatly appreciates her gifts. Our imaginations are powerful. Sometimes we need to reimagine what life looks like without another person, to see ourselves with a relationship or job or something else around which we built a picture of the happy life. Ignatian imaginative prayer can help us see different possibilities from those we considered before a loss.

Jesus' Passion and Our Own

Sometimes the meaning of our suffering needs a new narrative. Here again, the resources of Ignatian prayer can help. Through looking at Jesus' life, we might find new ways to tell the story of what our own suffering means.

In the *Spiritual Exercises*, Ignatius has us spend time with Jesus' passion. It is a way for us to learn the story of Jesus' suffering and to consider how we might retell our own story in light of his. We can sit with Jesus, pray with Jesus in the Garden of Gethsemane, be with his mother and his friends at the foot of the cross, and accompany him in all that he experiences. By praying with Jesus' passion, whether by imagining different moments in the Gospel story or the traditional stations of the cross, we can enter a new kind of story about suffering itself. We learn, first of all, that God always wants to heal and bring us to new life, just as God raised up Jesus. We also can learn to comfort Jesus, to enter his pain and sorrow, and so allow him to enter our own. This experience of accompanying Jesus in his passion can be powerful.

Many years ago, I underwent a deep clinical depression. Despite the depression, most of the time I was able to function and to hide my interior state from many of my colleagues and students. One Palm Sunday, in prayer I accompanied the wounded Jesus and showed him all my wounds. He stood across from me, battered and bruised, bleeding in places. There I stood without any bruises but with what then felt like unending internal pain. I said to Jesus, "Your wounds are visible, but mine are invisible. No one else can see them." Jesus replied, "By my stripes, your wounds are healed." I recognized his promise of healing, one that was eventually fulfilled. Then Jesus took the tiny glass vessel used to hold holy water near the altar at Mass and caught my tears in the vessel. I realized that my tears were precious to God, seen by God. God knows and accepts our tears. My tears were gifts that God could use and offer along with the gift of his own blood.

Mary Magdalene and Resurrection

We might even have to tell new narratives about what our own experiences of the Resurrection look like. A figure who has been helpful to me in thinking about this is Mary Magdalene. The encounter between Jesus and Mary Magdalene is a bit puzzling. This story is read at the beginning of the Easter Octave each year, a time when we celebrate the

Resurrection with great joy. And yet so much seems to be missing from the story. The tomb is empty. Initially, Mary does not recognize Jesus. Even after she does, Jesus tells her not to "hold on to him" because he has not yet ascended to the Father. This is all the more confusing because in the same Gospel, Jesus invites Thomas to put his hands into his wounds, to feel and to touch Jesus. Why does Jesus seemingly turn away from Mary Magdalene precisely at her moment of need for reconnection?

I have come to understand Jesus' words not as a "turning away" but rather as a different kind of "turning toward." Jesus calls Mary by her name, and it is in hearing her name that she first recognizes Jesus. Her response, though, is to call him "teacher" (*rabbi*). Perhaps his speaking to her and telling her not to greet him and touch him in the usual way is a response to her naming him as teacher. Mary, like all the disciples, is accustomed to seeing Jesus heal, teach, and act at the center of the ministry of the apostles. She is used to being the student. Perhaps she wishes to resume this relationship of teacher and student, as it is the one most familiar and the one by which she can best name Jesus. In so many of our broken relationships where we desire reconciliation, one desire might be to go back to a specific time in the past when the relationship was different: before the end of a marriage when the relationship was still passionate and harmonious, or when a friendship expressed love in a particular way.

Jesus, though, gives Mary different instructions. He tells her not to cling to him but to go and tell the others that he is risen. Mary listens and goes out. For this reason, Mary is often called the "apostle to the apostles" in speaking to them of the risen Lord. Jesus, in effect, gives Mary a mission. His telling her not to cling to him is not his turning away from her but rather turning toward her, becoming even *more* attentive to who Mary really is. Jesus is moving her forward into the future rather than back into the past, when he also instructs her to go and tell the good news. I like to imagine that, later on, Jesus and Mary meet again, but this time she understands her new place in God's redemptive work.

What might this look like concretely in our own lives? For me, it has meant not only reconciling with others but also embracing my own mission in the world. I have learned that, like Mary Magdalene, I have a role to play in God's world and that a manifestation of the Resurrection after the Passion is each of us living out this mission. Jesus is here not only to rescue me but also to empower me to be his friend and companion.

Each of us must also learn what it means for us to live into the future and not according to our old models and images.

Perhaps it is an entirely new way of envisioning a vocation such as religious life or marriage or leaving behind the form in which we once knew God, not "holding on" to God in this old form but being willing to go out and live that vocation in a new way so that, like Mary Magdalene, we might meet him on the way again.

Over the course of life, our imagery of God often changes as we grow. Perhaps, as children, we imagined God as an old man with a beard living up in heaven, high above the clouds. Later, we might imagine God as a friend or lover, as a comforting mother, or in more symbolic forms, as in the image of the dove leading me, as an image of the Holy Spirit. Over my life, my image of myself may also shift, as I give up certain images of who I am in favor of others. Perhaps I imagine myself in terms of my career or as a wife or mother but later discover that my deepest identity in God is not reducible to any of those images. Likewise, when I forgive another, or experience forgiveness, my image of another may also expand beyond my earlier, narrower constructions.

We are recipients of the gift of the Holy Spirit, and this Spirit has given us a mission to enact in this world. Our lives will develop and expand beyond the narratives we have constructed for ourselves so far. How can you let go of your old story of how your life will look and allow God to construct a new narrative with you?

Here are some ways to reflect on and pray over what might need changing in our own narratives.

- Write out your own story of what happened. Honor your story and recognize its legitimacy. Then imagine what the other person's story might be. If she or he were to write it out, what might that story look like? Perhaps several days or weeks after writing these different accounts, ask God to help you rewrite the narrative about the events. How do you and God *together* want to tell your story?

- As a gardener and nature lover, I have often found observation of plants and their decay, death, and new life over the change of seasons to be a helpful metaphor. Take a walk outdoors and notice where your own interior experiences now are found in the natural world. Is this a time of quiet, hidden growth? Big, splashy flowers? Or the silent and unobservable dormant rest of roots underground, still awaiting resurrection?

- Pray imaginatively with the scene where Jesus meets Mary Magdalene. Imagine the scene of the tomb in the garden. Look into the empty tomb. What does the absence of Jesus feel like? Where is Jesus now? What words does Jesus want to offer you? How does Jesus express to you an invitation to new life?

- If you are involved in a process of reconciliation, reflect on this short parable of Jesus. "The kingdom of heaven is like yeast that a woman took and mixed in with three measures of flour until all of it was leavened" (Matthew 13:33). Yeast is tiny, but with time, the dough into which it is mixed rises. Sometimes the smallest gestures of reconciliation, plus time, can help grow into a larger process of healing. What small gestures is God inviting you to make? Where is God asking you to let go and give God time to let the dough rise?

Prayer: New Life

Lord, help me live into new life.
As green shoots sprout up from spring ground,
As rain restores water to dry earth,
As light rises over dusk and darkness,
Enlighten, strengthen, and restore my soul.

Help me to unclench my tight fists that cling
To old relationships or worn out identities.
When I peer into the empty tomb,
Let me see but not stay.

Turn me around, convert my heart and mind,
That I may walk along new paths and see with
        opened eyes.
Breathe new life into my lungs, hands, feet, voice.

Awaken me,
Surprise me,
Free me,
That I might delight in you and proclaim your
        love anew.

—Marina Berzins McCoy

Step Eight

Embrace the Child but Become the Parent

In his book *The Return of the Prodigal Son*, Henri Nouwen looks at the parable of the prodigal son through a series of reflections on each of the three main figures in the story, especially as represented in a Rembrandt painting. Nouwen notes that at times we are like the son who returns home, who needs forgiveness. We sin and we look for a return to the loving arms of God, who embraces us exactly as we are. Sometimes, though, we are also like the older brother, who resents the return of the wayward son and wonders why his father has not been celebrating him, when he has always been upright. Nouwen notes that this son, too, has also been lost in his own way; his resentment reflects a "moralistic intensity" that does not allow him to share in others' joy.[12] The older son, too, must learn that he is loved by his father, not for the good deeds he has accomplished but simply because he is his father's beloved one. Last, there is the figure of the father, who welcomes home the prodigal son and tries to reassure the eldest son of his love too.

The prodigal son is so named because he is a spendthrift. After asking for his inheritance in advance and leaving behind his father's home, he spends all his funds until he is reduced to eating pig feed. For a Jewish audience especially, for whom pigs were not kosher to eat, this must have been a striking image of how low the son had fallen. He decides to return to his father, thinking that he will, at best, be allowed to become a servant to his father. We can only imagine the thoughts and feelings such a son would have, especially in days before cell phones and e-mail, with no way to get a reliable message home in advance. His arrival will be the first sign of his return after years away. I imagine that such a person would struggle with anxiety, fear, and shame. He has no claim on his father's house. As Nouwen notes, asking for his inheritance in advance was tantamount to wishing his father were dead. Perhaps he wonders whether he will travel all the way home only to be turned away at the door, or not even to have his knock answered. We, too, can doubt and struggle with whether God or others whose care we desire can fully receive us as we are.

Yet the son must have had a spark of hope to make the journey home, a hope grounded in a sense of trust in who his father was. As Jesus presents the story, even before the son reaches the house, his father sees him and rushes out to meet him. His father embraces him and welcomes him back not as a servant but as a lost son who has been found again. The father throws a party and arranges for the best possible food with the fatted calf.

This parable reveals at least three qualities of God's mercy with us. First, even before we seek out God's forgiveness, God's love awaits us. God does not need for us to make the first move but is like a loving parent who has been waiting for us all along. Second, God's mercy embraces the whole of our experience. The father of the story embraced his son, who was likely a mess physically, emotionally, and spiritually. God wants to hear and to hold all our emotions and experiences, not only the admirable ones but also the messy ones. God's arms are large enough to hold all our experiences, however powerful our anger, grief, upset, sadness, or disappointments may be. Third, God's mercy culminates not with simple forgiveness but with celebration. The father puts a ring and a robe on his son who has returned and then throws him a party. Mercy does not end with the acceptance of the past but with the celebration of the future.

I remember reading Nouwen's book one Lent when I was struggling to forgive a friend after a major conflict. My friend lived in a different part of the country and refused to engage in any kind of conversation or process of healing. On my own part, I had been reactive, overcommunicating and pushing my friend to relate in ways that were not respectful of a longer process. I identified with the prodigal son in the story, feeling acutely the places where I had reacted emotionally and wanting to be received despite my emotional outburst during a conflict. Yet despite my reaching out, no response was forthcoming. I felt needy and rejected in my neediness. How I longed to be that prodigal daughter, embraced by someone who waited for me even before I reached the door. Reading further into Nouwen's account, I then read this:

> "A child does not remain a child. A child becomes an adult. An adult becomes father and mother. When the prodigal son returns home, he returns not to remain a child, but to claim his sonship and become a father himself. As the returned child of God who is invited to resume my place in my Father's home, the challenge now, yes, the call, is to become the Father myself." (Nouwen, *Return of the Prodigal Son*, 118–19)

I know that God spoke to me through this passage because I recognized that inside me was a resistance to taking up my experience and allowing it to shape me into the kind of friend or mentor I could be for other people. I had been spending so much emotional energy on wanting to be akin to a child that I had overlooked the ways I was being asked to be a consistent and faithful friend to others. Although I could not control how my friend regarded me or make him embody the love of God for which I longed, I could seek to embody fidelity in my own relationships, personally and professionally.

Once I took this invitation seriously, I realized that there were many things I had learned from being on the hurt side of this relationship, wisdom I could bring to bear in my relationships with others as a spouse, friend, teacher, prison volunteer, and spiritual director. For example, I try to be a faithful ongoing presence at the prison that I visit and recognize that their ongoing hospitality to me and to other volunteers is an act of fidelity on their part. I am not a perfect friend, but I try to be there for these friends through their ups and downs and to love others in their imperfection even as they love me in mine. I hope to be the kind of mother who gives her adult children the right balance of freedom and a safe home to which they can return.

Any of us can become the prodigal mother or father—not through completely eliminating our desire to be the prodigal daughter or son but rather through allowing God to parent us and embrace us, so that we have the energy to grow up and give love to others in more mature ways. I once saw it phrased this way in an online meme: "Be the person that you needed to be when you were younger." Loving, more than being loved, is what frees us.

Here are some thoughts you can bring to prayer.

1. First, with whom do you most identify in the story of the prodigal son? Are you the son/daughter, the elder brother/sister, or the prodigal father/mother? Each of these figures in the story wants something, and in each case, it is not other human beings alone but God who can provide it. What desires do you now have at this point in the process? What desires do you want to bring to God? Can you do that now in your prayer?

2. Pray with the story of the prodigal son imaginatively from the point of view of one of the sons/daughters. However, instead of imagining among the characters the human being with whom you are in conflict, imagine God's presence as the prodigal father or mother. If you are one of the sons/daughters, how does God want

to comfort and embrace you in this situation? What does God want to celebrate and appreciate in you?

3. Pray with the story of the prodigal son but this time from the point of view of the father or mother. Where have you been an agent of love and reconciliation in the world? For whom or with whom might you be invited to enact faithful love or reconciliation in your life now? Imagine that God's embrace of you has now given you energy to go on to love and to embrace others.

Desmond Tutu's Prayer for Peace

O God, all holy one, you are our Mother and our Father and we are your children. Open our eyes and our hearts so that we may be able to discern your work in the universe. And be able to see your features in every one of your children. May we learn that there are many paths but all lead to you. Help us to know that you have created us for family, for togetherness, for peace, for gentleness, for compassion, for caring, for sharing.

May we know that you want us to care for one another as those who know that they are sisters and brothers, members of the same family, your family, the human family. Help us to beat our swords into plowshares and our spears into pruning hooks, so that we may be able to live in peace and harmony, wiping away the tears from the eyes of those who are less fortunate than ourselves. And may we know war no more, as we strive to be what you want us to be: your children.

Amen.

Resting Point

Consider a Ritual of Closure

Now is a good time to stop and assess your situation. To what extent have prayer, time, and God's grace moved you closer to forgiveness? Give thanks to God for these gifts, even if it seems as though there is still a long way to go. Are there steps that you wish to retrace or prayers that have felt helpful and worth repeating? Now is a good time to go back to those prayers or actions that have been most fruitful in moving you closer to forgiveness and freedom. Do you need a break and time to put down your pack and rest awhile? It is okay to do so. Or is it time to place a degree of closure on the process of forgiveness? There is no rush to do so. There is no timeline that you must superimpose on the process of forgiveness.

Sometimes forgiveness has seemed like a very long hike indeed. Sometimes, though, the Resurrection sneaks up on us. I can think of an instance in which I struggled to forgive another's hurtful action. I remember talking with a Jesuit spiritual director about how frustrated I was that I was doing all the "right things" to try to love and let go of past hurts but found myself feeling unable to do it. My director helpfully suggested that perhaps forgiveness would not look like the result of a set process. Perhaps forgiveness would not be the result of a particular moment of prayer or a heartfelt moment of interpersonal reconciliation between myself and another. Maybe one day, he said, I would simply be occupied with other events and relationships in my life and suddenly notice, hey, I really *have* forgiven and let go. Hearing my director's wise words helped relieve some pressure I had put on myself.

One spring, I decided to just stand back and dispassionately ask myself, "Am I happy this hour?" each hour of a day for the course of several days. To my surprise, I found that most of the time, I experienced genuine happiness and engagement with my family, work, and the larger world. Of course, there were moments of ordinary human sadness, but there were even more moments of joy. I realized that I had to shift my narrative about myself and the difficult events of my life. These experiences no longer defined me or seeped into my present. I had to give up the story I had been telling myself. I had to let go of the all-too-comfortable identity of being a victim. The Resurrection was already there, and yet it took me time to see, to taste, to sense its presence in and around me.

When Jesus meets the two disciples walking on the way to Emmaus after his resurrection, they are leaving behind Jerusalem. Jerusalem no longer holds the same promise it did before the Crucifixion. From the point of view of these friends of Jesus, there is nothing but failure. The Gospel tells us that when Jesus joins them, he walks with them, "but their eyes were kept from recognizing him" (Luke 24:16). Jesus is so near and is already fully resurrected. Yet they do not see.

Jesus asks these two friends what they are discussing. Cleopas responds, "Are you the only stranger in Jerusalem who does not know the things that have taken place there in these days?" (Luke 24:18). This is a humorous moment in the story because Jesus knows better than anyone what has happened, not only the events but also their meaning. Cleopas sees only partially, and his focus on the past blinds him to the reality of the Resurrection in the present.

It takes time to see the Resurrection. We may not see it until it has already been present for a while. We may find that one day we are still holding on to anger, hurt, or ill thinking and another day notice that we really have arrived at a place of forgiveness. Perhaps it is even a surprise to us. We then recognize that this is a grace and that the Lord has been here. In this act of recognition, we may discover freedom and warmth in our hearts, where before there were only disappointment and pain. The Lord has touched us, yet we notice only in the afterglow.

Fr. Eamon Tobin writes, "There is a difference between the *forgiveness* of a hurt and the *total healing* of a hurt."[13] Even if we still feel some aches and pains over the past, we may have reached the point of forgiveness. Healing helps us set the conditions to make forgiveness possible. But sometimes the very decision to forgive makes healing more possible. That healing may still take a long time to come to its completion. It took time for the two disciples to see Jesus in the breaking of the bread and the breaking open of Scripture. It was a long walk.

When we are ready, some kind of ritual that symbolizes closure can help. At the oceanside retreat house at Eastern Point in Gloucester, Massachusetts, that I often attend for a weeklong silent retreat, large boulders form the majority of the landscape at the seashore. Retreatants here have the practice of placing smaller rocks atop these larger ones, perhaps to symbolize a prayer intention or perhaps to represent a person or a relationship. Other retreatants can sometimes be seen throwing rocks off the sides of these boulders into the ocean, perhaps as an attempt to embody letting go of someone or something. A common experience on the Camino pilgrimage to Santiago de Compostela is to bring a stone to leave at the Cruz de Ferro, or Iron Cross. It is the highest point along the French Way. People leave rocks for many reasons: to remember a family member who has died or to let go of a sense of guilt for past sins. This ritual allows many people to first carry their burdens in the form of a stone and then to release them at the foot of the cross as a way to let go of them and give them over to God's mercy.

We can be creative with these rituals and find our own. A man I know mourned the loss of his fiancée after she left him for another man: He created a paper boat on which he had written both the gifts and negatives of their relationship. He went to a local pond and set the paper boat afloat to bid her farewell. Although he had not fully worked through all his feelings about the relationship's end, he was able to ritualize the end of the relationship and to express the *desire to forgive and to let go* through that little paper boat. We can create our own rituals that formalize a decision to forgive, even if our emotions still need time to be processed and our hearts need further time to heal. This is okay. We can make the decision to forgive, yet recognize that the flow of feelings may continue to come and go. The recurrence of feelings does not remove the reality of the act of forgiveness.

Here are some ideas for embarking on a process of closure.

- Consider a ritual to express the act of forgiveness, one shared between you and God. Above, the suggestions of a paper boat or a rock offered to God on a hike or journey are two examples. However, other possibilities abound: we might light a candle and name the gifts and pains of a relationship, end with a prayer for the other person, and then extinguish the candle.

- You might choose to write a letter to express forgiveness of another, without asking anything in return. In some cases, sending the letter might be a first step toward reconciliation. In cases where a letter may not be welcome or helpful, we can still write the letter but then perhaps shred it or let it burn in the fireplace, to release these ideas to God.

- It is intriguing that one of the two disciples on the road to Emmaus is named (Cleopas) while the other is left unnamed. It is as though we are being invited to imagine: *Who is this other unnamed friend, for us?* Who have been the friends, mentors, guides, or other companions who have walked with you on the path of forgiveness? How are they also part of the Resurrection story? Offer gratitude to God for their presence.

- To love is to wish the good of another and to desire his or her happiness. Pray simply for the happiness of the other person. Let this wish for their happiness wash over an image of the other person as you hold their image in your imagination.

An Irish Blessing

May the road rise to meet you.
May the wind be always at your back.
May the sun shine warm upon your face,
The rain fall soft upon your fields,
And until we meet again,
May God hold you in the palm of his hand.

Step Nine

Cultivate Habits of Mercy

To choose to forgive might seem like the last step on the path of forgiveness. And yet, to forgive is not the last step. Rather, forgiveness takes us only partway down the path upon which God is leading us. When we enter the process of forgiving another person, we may find that our view of the world and human relationships changes. We may feel ourselves drawn into *choosing lives that are committed to mercy*, beyond the individual instance of forgiveness that has challenged us.

My favorite definition of mercy is by theologian James Keenan, SJ, who names it as "the willingness to enter into the chaos of another."[14] To enter the chaos of another is to allow ourselves to be touched by the plight of others and to risk entering a degree of the powerlessness that is involved in solidarity. Mercy is wider than forgiveness, for mercy includes actions such as the corporal and spiritual works of mercy: feeding the hungry, visiting those who are in prison, bearing patiently with the faults of others, for example. An essential part of mercy includes forgiveness, but mercy does not end there. The process of forgiveness is one that can lead us to our own conversion of heart, turning our "heart[s] of stone" into "heart[s] of flesh" (Ezekiel 36:26). Our stony hearts get broken up and softened in part through encountering the suffering and difficulties of others and placing ourselves in solidarity with them. If Tom serves by tutoring in a school for children who lack sufficient educational resources, he may come to feel genuine heartbreak if he learns that some of the students are hungry as a result of poverty. This may motivate him not only to serve but also to seek ways to address childhood hunger more widely in his community. Mercy includes coming to know and to build relationships with those who are in need; when we enter these kinds of situations, we bring our life experiences with us.

Our encounter with mercy in the form of forgiving and being forgiven can also inform how we practice mercy in its wider ways. Pope Francis says in *Gaudete et Exsultate*, "Giving and forgiving means reproducing in our lives some small measure of God's perfection, which gives and forgives super-abundantly."[15]

How do we become people of mercy? Ignatius encourages us to look to the life of Jesus as a model to imitate. Where do we see Jesus act with mercy? Mercy informs nearly every action that Jesus undertakes in his ministry. For example, we see Jesus approach the woman who is about to be stoned for adultery. Instead of condemning her or stoning her, he encourages those who are about to throw stones to be merciful. His entryway into their mercy is to say, "Let anyone among you who is without sin be the first to throw a stone at her" (John 8:7). No one throws any stones, and the woman is free to walk away.

I once heard an old joke that tells this same story, but instead of ending with the woman leaving, the story ends when a single stone is thrown. The punch line of the joke is to have Jesus say, "Hey, Ma, I told you not to bother me when I am at work!" Of course, the joke references the Catholic teaching that Mary was without sin—as well as the stereotype of mothers who desire overinvolvement in their adult children's lives!

But the joke raises a good point, in a way: There *was* yet another person who was present, sinless, and who could have condemned the woman: Jesus himself. Yet Jesus says,

"Neither do I condemn you" (John 8:11). This shows us that the reason not to condemn others for their sin goes much deeper than acknowledging our own need for forgiveness. We see that mercy is God's very nature. Mercy is an aspect of divine love. For us, too, the question as to whether to be merciful might begin with recognizing our own need for mercy. But it goes further. *Lives of mercy eventually become a participation in divine love, a mode of sharing in friendship with God to heal the world.* We are invited to follow Jesus in enacting mercy in our world.

I find it remarkable that when Jesus heals and forgives, we never hear him ask for reasons or explanations for past actions. There is *no* parable that goes anything like this: "The man sitting at the side of the dusty road begged Jesus for mercy. 'Have mercy on me, a sinner!' Then Jesus approached the man and said, 'I might, but first tell me, why did you sin? Perhaps if your explanation is good enough, then I will forgive you. What's the story?'"

Instead, the pattern is much more often like this one: "Just then some people were carrying a paralytic lying on a bed. When Jesus saw their faith, he said to the paralytic, 'Take heart, son; your sins are forgiven' (Matthew 9:2). And Jesus heals him."

That's it—other than the complaints of the passersby, who say Jesus is committing blasphemy by forgiving! Jesus' encounter with the man is simple and to the point. He heals, he forgives, and he says, "Stand up, take your bed and go to your home" (Matthew 9:6b).

Mercy is God's nature. Mercy is Jesus' *incarnate* nature: embodied in a real, living, breathing human being, and not only as an abstract force. What if mercy were also *our* deepest nature and at the heart of our truest selves, when we are united in friendship with God? Jesus tells us, "Be merciful, just as your Father is merciful" (Luke 6:36). He goes on to say, "A disciple is not above the teacher, but everyone who is fully qualified will be like the teacher" (Luke 6:40). We are invited to learn to love as God loves. Forgiveness is part of our training ground.

Cultivating Habits of Compassion

How do we get to the point of loving as God loves? We can *cultivate habits of compassion*. We become merciful people only by performing merciful actions. This means acting with forgiveness and compassion in all the small areas of life as well as the larger moments. I remember reading a story in the Boston news about a girl who had been shot accidentally in a gang shooting. She was paralyzed and in a wheelchair as a result of the violence. Nonetheless, in the courtroom, she offered forgiveness to the man who had shot her. I wondered what could have inspired someone so young to forgive another person? Something deep inside her, from God, must have inspired such an action. I also wondered what kind of a person she would become as an adult. Perhaps this was her first choice in life to decide to embark upon the path of mercy, and this was only the beginning of a life marked by mercy, forgiveness, and love. We, too, can decide what will be the starting point for us in developing habits of mercy. Where do you want to cultivate forgiveness? Where do you feel called to go serve?

If there has been progress in moving toward forgiveness, this is a gift for which to be thankful and on which to build. However, if the process has remained difficult, perhaps it is time to shift attention away from this one instance or event in need of forgiveness. Perhaps it's time to take a different path, one that will lead to the same final destination but by a different way. In cases where forgiveness seems beyond reach, consider instead embarking on another path that allows the practice of mercy and compassion. Perhaps this could mean volunteering at a soup kitchen, working on a parish project to benefit others, or participating in a pen-pal program with prisoners.

Embodied Compassion

Mercy is closely related to compassion. Henri Nouwen notes that there is a Greek term for compassion in the Gospels that is used to refer only to the experience of either Jesus or the Father: *splangchnizomai*. Nouwen writes, "The splangchna are the entrails of the body, or as we might say today, the guts. They are the place where our most intimate and intense emotions are located. They are the center from which both passionate love and passionate hate grow."[16] Nouwen argues that Jesus' experience of compassion went far beyond sympathy. It was a stance of solidarity, an act of entering the experience of what it is to be human, and a willingness to allow what was most vulnerable in Jesus to become engaged in his encounters with others.[17] Jesus stayed with others, remaining as a compassionate presence with them, never running from suffering, as so many of his disciples and friends later ran away from Jesus' own suffering and death.

Sometimes I think that we run away from reconciliation not because of a lack of empathy but because we have so much of it. At these times, we know that compassion for a person who has harmed us will touch us at a deep level. Ruth, a retired prison chaplain who mentored me in my prison ministry, likes to say, "Only hurt people hurt other people." Many men and women who are incarcerated for a crime speak of acknowledging the immense hurt they have suffered in their families or communities and growing to understand how their actions emerged out of these unhealed wounds. This is often true for anyone, not just prisoners. When we see others acting in anger, our desire to run away and to protect ourselves is natural. But when we are safe and no longer in harm's way, we still may avoid reconciliation because to allow ourselves to feel compassion for the wounds of another person touches us very deeply indeed, all the way to our "insides." I have found that my time visiting with and serving a community of prisoners also opened me up to greater self-compassion for my own limits, as well as compassion for others who have hurt or even abused me. When we cultivate habits of mercy, we find that we are changed by our own acts of mercy but also by those in the communities we visit.

Some of my own lessons about extending mercy have been learned from the men I have served at a state prison. One of them, Rick, writes this about mercy:

"I once thought the person exercising mercy has or feels they have some sort of power or authority over those they have been merciful to. But really, even those who appear powerless possess the power to grant or deny mercy. There's a common saying among prisoners about correctional officers, on whom we depend to be merciful. It is said that correctional officers were the kids that get picked on in school and now they are getting even by bullying people who can do nothing about it. Do we recognize our lack of mercy in such statements? . . . Perhaps they are trying to do a difficult job. . . . Empathy and understanding are frameworks for mercy regardless of convictions."[18]

Rick recognizes the humanity of correctional officers and the need for both "sides" in the prison system to show mercy and care for one another. Yes, we need to build up justice in our institutions, but justice is not enough. We also need to show mercy. This model inspires me to consider where in the institutions I belong to I can recognize my call to both give and receive mercy.

To have empathy for the one who has betrayed me, or even abused me, can be gut-wrenching. To recognize that another person who has hurt me may have acted out of deep, unhealed wounds is to let their pain touch mine in the moment of empathy for those wounds. To allow myself to be vulnerable to these feelings can even feel scary.

What, then, allows us to stay with and hold these feelings of compassion? We do not have to hold them alone. We hold them with God by allowing God to be present to our situation with us. Other people in our community, perhaps others who have experienced the same or similar harms, or perhaps those who are less touched by the situation and so have more energy to give us, can also stay with us as our allies. We do not have to travel the road of compassion alone.

The Flow of Divine Mercy

Mercy and compassion, then, are two sides of this divine love. On the one hand, there is the compassion that allows us to be touched even at the gut level, to experience deep empathy for a situation of wounding and suffering. On the other hand, there is a source of divine mercy that comes from an unquenchable love. The nineteenth-century Dominican priest Jean-Joseph Lataste, O.P., is best known for his compassionate visits with women imprisoned in Cadillac, France. Rather than see them as "fallen women," he recognized these women as God's beloved ones. My friend Ruth once shared with me an image from Lataste for how to reconcile this desire of God to enter human experience with God's perfection: overflowing water. Lataste said, "God thirsts: He is like a vase that is too full, with no means of pouring himself out on those around him. He thirsts, but as a torrent which, in its thirst, precipitates to find an abyss that it can fill with its waters."[19] We can enter the abundance of this divine "flow" and so find our way to a kind of compassion whereby it is safe to allow ourselves to feel a wide range of emotions, even to be touched by the pain that leads others to act in hurtful or sinful ways. I believe that we have access to join this river of divine love, to access our capacity to show mercy through accessing the wider flow of love that God offers to every one of us.

John Eagan, SJ, proposes this simple prayer: "How do you, Lord, look at me? What do you feel in your heart for me?"[20] When we allow ourselves to see, feel, and receive the love of God in ourselves, we learn not only of our own belovedness. We also find the energy to extend this same love toward others. Pope Benedict XVI in his encyclical *God Is Love* (*Deus Caritas Est*) writes that every human being longs for a "look of love" that affirms his worth and well-being. We as humans are also encouraged to provide that "look of love" to others.[21] We can do this, though, only when we have first been the recipient of unconditional, patient, merciful love.

Pope Francis was once asked, "Why does God not tire of forgiving us?" He answered, "Because he is God, because he is mercy, and because mercy is the first attribute of God. The name of God is mercy."[22] We are made in God's image, and so we, too, are invited to be agents of mercy.

Jesus and Peter Reconcile

How did Peter, who initially betrayed Jesus, go on to live the life of an apostle who was even willing to die for the faith?

Peter was transformed by his experience of the Resurrection. The Gospel according to John may give us some insight into how this can take place.

> When they had finished breakfast, Jesus said to Simon Peter, "Simon, son of John, do you love me more than these?" He said to him, "Yes, Lord; you know that I love you." Jesus said to him, "Feed my lambs." A second time he said to him, "Simon, son of John, do you love me?" Simon Peter answered him, "Yes, Lord; you know that I love you." Jesus said to him, "Tend my sheep." He said to him the third time, "Simon, son of John, do you love me?" Peter felt hurt because he said to him a third time, "Do you love me?" And he said to him, "Lord, you know everything; you know that I love you."
>
> —John 21:15–17

This interchange between Jesus and Peter is so tender. Jesus asks Peter multiple times, "Do you love me?" and we see the reiteration of love, back and forth between Jesus and Peter. It is a deeply reconciling moment. As many commentators have suggested, Jesus seems to offer the three questions as a way to allow Peter to affirm what he denied before, when he denied his friendship with Jesus three times before the cock crowed. Peter gets another chance to give his true answer to Jesus.

The Greek used in this passage makes the situation a little more nuanced, though. The first two times that Jesus asks

Peter, "Do you love me?" Jesus uses the Greek verb associated with agapic love, or a love that is unconditional or even self-sacrificing. *Agape* is a kind of love that looks to the good of the other. Later Christian thinkers choose *agape* as the best Greek word to communicate how God loves us and as a model for how we ought to love our neighbor: with a love that encompasses all without condition. Aquinas defines it as the "effective willing of the good of another." It's doing what is best for the other and not for oneself.

Peter answers Jesus' question, "Do you love me [agapically]?" affirmatively: "You know that I love you." But Peter responds with the verb for love associated with friendship love (*philia*). *Philia* is the love that we have for our friends, although it can also be used a little more extensively than the English word for friendship. *Philia* is a kind of love that concerns a personal and felt connection to another person. If you are my friend, I love you not just because you are a human being. I love you because, in some way, we connect in a particular and special way. *Agape* can be one way, as when I love my enemy. But *philia* is reciprocal. Like the interchange and give-and-take between Jesus' and Peter's language here, *philia* requires that both friends love one another.

Given that Peter has betrayed Jesus, it makes perfect sense to me that Peter would hesitate to tell Jesus that he loves him with an agapic love. After all, Peter did not exhibit that kind of love for Jesus when he denied him and ran away in fear. Rather, Jesus exhibited that kind of love for Peter in his self-giving death and his forgiveness. Peter is being honest in not claiming to be better than he is. But he still tells Jesus that he loves him: Peter loves Jesus as his beloved friend, as a person who matters to him, even if he lacks the perfectly self-less love that Peter probably wishes he had. Jesus asks him the same question a second time using the term *agape*, and Peter again reiterates his love for Jesus, again using the term *philia*.

The third time the question and answer change, but it is not Peter who changes his language. It's Jesus. Jesus asks Peter, "Do you love me?" And this time he uses the verb associated with *philia*, or friendship love. And Peter affirms his *philia* for Jesus.

What is going on here? I have two suggestions. One is that Peter is admitting that he loves Jesus as an imperfect and sinful human being, and Jesus' change to his question the third time is a way to show Peter that he doesn't demand perfect, unfailing love from Peter. They still have a relationship even in Peter's imperfection, even in Peter's being only a human being and not a god. In all the limitations that come along with being human, Jesus and Peter remain friends.

A second suggestion is that Peter is standing somewhat firm with Jesus in affirming his particular friendship for Jesus when he refuses to use the word *agape* and sticks to the term *philia*. Perhaps Peter refuses to use the word for agapic loving not only because it is not accurate with respect to his own shortcomings but also because Peter is good at identifying something else significant about how he feels about Jesus: Jesus is not just loved because he is God. Peter loves Jesus because Jesus is his friend, because they have a shared history over time that is distinctive.

Jesus' third question then might be a response to Peter, to affirm the friendship between them. Yes, Jesus dies for everyone and his resurrection is for all, and Peter's ministry will also be a ministry for "all." But Jesus' humanity has not disappeared in the Resurrection, and it does not disappear when Peter takes up his ministry of agapic love. Peter still loves his friend Jesus in his particularity. Perhaps his answer "You know that I love you" is, in part, a question posed back to Jesus: do you love me (Peter) as a friend despite all that has transpired? Now that Jesus is resurrected and appears different, does that particularity of care between them remain?

We might see Jesus' asking the question the third time with the verb for friendship-love as a clear yes. Jesus loves Peter as a friend and invites his friendship. Jesus loves Peter not simply because he fits into the category of "human being." Jesus loves Peter in all his particularity: for his gifts, his weaknesses, his strengths, even his little quirks. He still loves Peter for the history and the story of friendship that exists between them.

Jesus loves each person this way too. God does not love us just because we are human or even because we are Christian. God loves and appreciates each of us in our particularity and in all the little distinctive ways in which we each know and live out a certain, concrete, unrepeated history with him. Jesus is also affirming the good of loving one another in such a truly human way. It's good to love "humanity," but beware of the person who loves "humanity" but doesn't love his or her family or friends! For it is in our messily human and particular relationships that the most difficult and also the most rewarding loving takes place.

The passage ends with Jesus' allusion to Peter's own crucifixion for the sake of the faith. So, we get a little reversal at the end of the story: Jesus knows that Peter can and does love agapically, even though Peter does not recognize his capacity to do so right now.

Perhaps the message is that these two kinds of love, *agape* and *philia*, are more intertwined than many philosophers like to think. Jesus' agapic love for us makes loving our hard-to-love neighbor easier. But also, our friendship with Jesus and friendship with one another are interconnected. Jesus and Peter provide a model for how to be friends with one another. Jesus invites Peter—and us—not only to the drama of the cross but also into the great drama of everyday love: "Come, follow me."[23]

Here are some further suggestions for prayer and prayerful action.

1. Spend time simply resting in the gaze of love that God wants to offer you. Perhaps it is the face of Jesus or of his mother, Mary. If imagining their faces proves difficult, I have found it helpful to simply remember the "look of love" that a real, concrete person in my life has given to me. Perhaps the face of a parent or grandparent, favorite aunt or uncle, encouraging mentor, or caring friend can embody the look of love that God wants us to receive. Allow the energy of that divine love and mercy to be received. Rest in it.

2. Pray with this look of love, but this time, imagine sending this love out to the person who has harmed you, like sunshine or a healing, warm ray of love. If this is difficult, practice by sending love to a stranger you have recently encountered in daily life but for whom you have no particular emotional attachment.[24]

3. Then try praying for your "enemy" later.

4. Choose to undertake a corporal or spiritual work of mercy. For example, perhaps you want to focus on care for those who need food or shelter by volunteering time or making this a focus of prayer for those who are homeless.

5. Walk with Jesus as Peter did. Where have you known friendship with God over the course of this process of forgiveness? Take time to review some of the key moments in which God has been present. Where do you, like Peter, want to go and bring this friendship with Jesus back into the wider world?

Suscipe

Take, Lord, and receive all my liberty,
my memory, my understanding,
and my entire will,
All I have and call my own.
You have given all to me.
To you, Lord, I return it.
Everything is yours; do with it what you will.
Give me only your love and your grace,
that is enough for me.

—St. Ignatius of Loyola

Step Ten

Celebrate

In the parable of the prodigal son, the homecoming ends with a party. The father who has embraced his son upon his return announces that there will be a celebration. It will be a lavish one. The fatted calf is slaughtered, and people don their party clothes. I imagine that the best wine was served, with many visitors invited to celebrate. Perhaps the prodigal son met childhood friends he had not seen in years. Perhaps the family invited others who needed the connection of a community for their own reasons. The parable reminds us that the aim and end goal of forgiveness is not only to forgive but also to celebrate in community with one another.

Celebrations of love are wonderful: weddings, engagements, homecomings. And yet, not everyone is always ready to celebrate. In the parable of the prodigal son, the eldest son holds back. He feels resentful and angry that such a party was never held for him, when he has always tried to be good and do the right thing. We can imagine that the older son is tempted not to join the party. Perhaps today he would be the person at work who goes back to his office to be "productive" while the holiday party is taking place on another floor. We imagine that he puts on his noise-canceling headphones so that he does not have to hear the music of celebration; he chooses to look at his screen rather than at his colleagues' faces.

But this is not God's perspective. Like the father in the prodigal son parable, God does not limit forgiveness to the remittal of sins or even the embrace between father and son. It is wonderful when forgiveness leads to an embrace, whether real or metaphorical. In broken relationships, we long for the place where "righteousness and peace will kiss each other" (Psalm 85:10). When this happens, whether interpersonally or in our own hearts, there is cause to celebrate, because forgiveness leads us back to living in love. Reconciliation allows us to be embraced by God in the wideness of God's even vaster love.

But there's more; the embrace between myself and the person with whom I have reconciled is not the end of the story. The end of this parable is the celebration in a wider community. Jesus shows us that this is how God thinks about forgiveness and reconciliation: as a movement that enables us to love more widely, to get up on the dance floor, and to dance the dance of love with more and more people. Forgiveness frees, but it is not only a freedom *from* resentment and anger but also freedom with a purpose: a *freedom to love*. Nouwen writes that God not only offers forgiveness and reconciliation but also "wants to lift up these gifts as a source of joy for all who witness them" (p. 113). Reconciliation is not all seriousness. It is an occasion for celebrating.

Contemplating Divine Love

At the end of the *Spiritual Exercises*, Ignatius suggests that retreatants pray the Contemplation to Attain the Love of God. In it, I consider all the gifts that God has given me, ranging from the personal talents I have to the gifts of family, relationships, and material goods that have helped me become the person I am. I meditate on how God tirelessly labors for me and works on my behalf in all things. At the end, I return all these gifts to God so that God can use them in whatever way God desires.

One way to bring this process of forgiving to a close is to pray with these same kinds of ideas. I might begin by thinking of different examples I know of those who have undertaken the work of forgiveness and reconciliation: Jesus, but perhaps also others such as Nelson Mandela, Martin Luther King Jr, or other famous figures. Perhaps I can think of individuals known to me more personally who are "saints of forgiveness," who accompany me on my own path of forgiving.

I might next consider this: What gifts have I received in undertaking this process of forgiveness? Even if it is not complete, what have I learned? How have I been graced?

This work takes place with God's assistance. I might next consider how God has labored on my behalf in this process of forgiveness. Who or what has God placed on my path to facilitate it? What moments in prayer or personal reflection have led me closer to forgiveness? What human conversations did God work through to bring me to this new place?

I last offer this back to God so that God can use the good of this work for peace and forgiveness in whatever ways God might want to in the future. I can only guess how God might want to use these gifts, but I offer to God my openness to using them in whatever way God desires.

We don't have celebration parties when we forgive and reconcile, but maybe we should. How can we celebrate, and what might it look like, to take this celebration out into the wider world? We celebrate this reconciling love every time we go to Eucharist. We also can celebrate reconciliation when we break bread together in everyday life: in meals shared with others when we come to the table together. Maybe this means sharing Thanksgiving dinner with the family member with whom there has been some kind of reconciliation. Perhaps it means spreading the forgiving love that is hidden and known only between you and God with others in the wider community.

In the Gospel stories where Jesus multiplies the loaves, Jesus gives us a model for how to live out the life of apostolic community in the feeding of the five thousand, an event with many resonances to Eucharist (Mark 6:34–44). Jesus takes up five loaves and two fish and gives them to his disciples to divide among the people. Jesus has just finished preaching to the crowd. He feeds them both with his words and with the bread. But he does not feed them alone, without any assistance, despite his miraculous powers. Instead, Jesus invites us to take up this work of feeding others along with him. We might think of this feeding of others as deadly serious, but this would be a mistake. Jesus threw a dinner party for five thousand people and invited us to spread the joy with others.

Jesus tells Simon (Peter) a short parable about two debtors that can help us better understand this divine perspective on forgiveness:

"A certain creditor had two debtors; one owed five hundred denarii, and the other fifty. When they could not pay, he canceled the debts for both of them. Now which of them will love him more?" Simon answered, "I suppose the one for whom he canceled the greater debt." And Jesus said to him, "You have judged rightly."

—Luke 7:41–43

Jesus' parable about the moneylender is a clear affirmation of God's love for sinners. But even more important, Jesus' story explains that the loved sinner may love God even more ardently than the person who has always believed herself to be a good and virtuous person, not in need of forgiveness and healing. Here, Jesus turns conventional judgments upside down. Whereas we might normally think that the person who is virtuous and has his life "together" is more likely to be a loving person, Jesus suggests it is not always the case. Sometimes the one who sins and repents, who knows God's love and his need for it, will love even more. And this willingness to love transparently, authentically, and lavishly is something in which God takes *delight*.

Loving Life in Its Messiness

We see an instance of this kind of lavish love and Jesus' reception of it when a woman enters a house where Jesus is having dinner. She anoints his feet with expensive, perfumed oil:

A woman in the city, who was a sinner, having learned that he was eating in the Pharisee's house, brought an alabaster jar of ointment. She stood behind him at his feet, weeping, and began to bathe his feet with her tears and to dry them with her hair. Then she continued kissing his feet and anointing them with the ointment. Now when the Pharisee who had invited him saw it, he said to himself, "If this man were a prophet, he would have known who and what kind of woman this is who is touching him—that she is a sinner."

—Luke 7:37–39

Others know this woman as a sinner. Yet she displays profligate love for Jesus, not only breaking open a bottle of scented oil and pouring it on his feet but even bending over to wipe off the excess with her hair. This woman's love for Jesus is extravagant, messy, emotional, and sensual. Although others witness her actions, her own focus seems to be entirely on Jesus, and Jesus' focus is entirely on her. She says nothing to the other dinner guests, provides no explanations, and makes no excuses. She is simply fully present to her love for Jesus and her desire to show that love to him without holding back. Jesus receives it all with joy. We also are invited to share our joy, in the context of our own families, communities, and everyday lives—with those who are in our lives here and now.

My friend Ruth likes to say, "God is in the mess." Love is messy. Love is not easily contained in nice, hermetically sealed containers. Love is made to be broken open, like the alabaster jar, or like the body of Jesus, and then shared with others. Sometimes, what looks like a disaster is really a deepening of love, just about to happen.

Jesus' parable about the two debtors contextualizes sin within a larger context of a relationship of love. Sin and its reconciliation are but moments in a much longer relationship between God and humanity. We live in the middle of a great love story with God—the greatest love story ever told because it continues to deepen. Sin never defines this relationship; love always does. God's love and desire to restore relationship are always the larger context, the bigger arms waiting to embrace, lift up, and help us dress up so that we can celebrate together.

Here are some ideas for how to pray to celebrate the lavishness of God's love and the fruits of forgiveness.

- The woman who anoints Jesus' feet not only pours precious oil on his feet but also pours out herself to Jesus. As you have walked down this road of forgiveness, what have you poured out of yourself to God? What more do you still want to pour out to God? How does God respond?

- Pray imaginatively with the image of Jesus feeding the five thousand. Jesus takes up several loaves and fishes and then redistributes them. Imagine that you are one of the disciples to whom he gives a loaf of bread to share. First, he feeds you, and then he asks you to go out and share this bread with others. Who is the next person with whom you want to break bread so that it may be further shared?

- Throw a party. Share dinner with a friend. Break bread with the homeless at a soup kitchen. Perhaps nobody but you and God know it is a celebration of forgiveness. Go ahead and celebrate.

- Imagine the image of the dance with which this book begins. Begin by imagining the scene for a while. What does the dance floor look like? In what kind of building is it being held? Who is there? What are you wearing? What songs are playing? Next, imagine yourself dancing with Jesus or Mary. Jesus or Mary then asks if there is someone else with whom you would like to dance. To whom do you turn next? When it is time to switch partners again, who is the next in line? Is the person you have forgiven out on the dance floor? If so, with whom is she or he now dancing?

Lord of the Dance

I danced in the morning when the world
        was begun,
And I danced in the moon and the stars and
        the sun,
And I came down from heaven and I danced on
        the earth.
At Bethlehem I had my birth.

Refrain: Dance, then, wherever you may be,
I am the Lord of the Dance, said he,
And I'll lead you all, wherever you may be,
And I'll lead you all in the Dance, said he.

I danced for the scribe and the Pharisee,
But they would not dance and they would not
        follow me;
I danced for the fishermen, for James and John;
They came with me and the Dance went on.

Refrain

I danced on the Sabbath and I cured the lame:
The holy people said it was a shame.
They whipped and they stripped and they hung me
        on high,
And they left me there on a cross to die.

Refrain

I danced on a Friday when the sky turned black;
It's hard to dance with the devil on your back.
They buried my body and they thought I'd gone;
But I am the Dance, and I still go on.

Refrain

They cut me down and I leapt up high;
I am the life that'll never, never die.
I'll live in you if you'll live in me;
I am the Lord of the Dance, said he.

Refrain

—Sydney Carter

Endnotes

1. My adaptation. Original text found on
   https://sacramentopilgrims.com/
   camino-prayers-poems/.

2. See Sean Salai, SJ, "The Psychological Insights of St.
   Ignatius Loyola," *America*, August 6, 2018,
   https://www.americamagazine.org/faith/2018/08/06/
   psychological-insights-st-ignatius-loyola.

3. Pope Francis, address to the world's priests, Chrism
   Mass, Holy Thursday, March 28, 2013, as found in
   National Catholic Reporter, October 29, 2013,
   https://www.ncronline.org/blogs/francis-chronicles/
   pope-s-quotes-smell-sheep.

4. James Martin, SJ, "The Virtues of Catholic Anger," *New
   York Times*, August 15, 2018,
   https://www.nytimes.com/2018/08/15/opinion/

the-virtues-of-catholic-anger.html, accessed August 15, 2018.

5. Thich Nhat Hanh, *Thich Nhat Hanh: Essential Writings*, ed. Robert Ellsberg (Maryknoll, NY: Orbis Books, 2001), 85.

6. "Ignatius's Three-Part Vision," https://www.ignatianspirituality.com/ignatian-prayer/ the-spiritual-exercises/ignatius-three-part-vision, accessed January 8, 2019.

7. Michael Himes, "Hope in a Wintry Season," https://www.bc.edu/bc-web/schools/stm/sites/encore/ main/2010/hope-wintery-season.html, accessed December 12, 2018.

8. I am grateful for Timothy Radcliffe, O.P.'s reflections on the disciples in the locked room as a resource for thinking about mission in *I Call You Friends* (London: Bloomsbury Continuum, 2013), 209–33.

9. Vinita Hampton Wright, "Four Reasons We Resist Letting Go," https://www.ignatianspirituality.com/ 24479/four-reasons-we-resist-letting-go, accessed August 3, 2018.

10. Rachel Naomi Remen, "Helping, Fixing or Serving?" https://www.uc.edu/content/dam/uc/honors/docs/ communityengagement/HelpingFixingServing.pdf.

11. See www.guestbookproject.org.

12. Henri J. M. Nouwen, *The Return of the Prodigal Son: A Story of Homecoming* (New York: Image Books/Doubleday, 1992), 71.

13. Eamon Tobin, *How to Forgive Yourself and Others*, rev. ed. (Liguori, MO: Liguori Publications, 1983, 1993, 2006), 3.

14. James F. Keenan, SJ, *The Works of Mercy: The Heart of Catholicism*, 3rd ed. (Lanham, MD: Rowman & Littlefield, 2017), 5.

15. Pope Francis, *Gaudete et Exsultate: On the Call to Holiness in Today's World* (Vatican City: Libreria Editrice Vaticana, 2018), no. 81, page 11.

16. Henri J. M. Nouwen, Donald P. McNeill, and Douglas A. Morrison, *Compassion: A Reflection on the Christian Life* (New York: Doubleday/Image Books, 1983), 14.

17. Ibid., 15–16.

18. Bethany House, ed., *Mirrors of Mercy* (Holts Summit, MO: Quail Valley Publishing, 2016), 60.

19. Marie Jean-Joseph Lataste, O.P., *Excerpts from the Writings of Marie Jean-Joseph Lataste*, section 22.

20. Michael Harter, SJ, ed., *Hearts on Fire* (Chicago: Loyola Press, 1993, 2004), 85.

21. Benedict XVI, *God Is Love* (Washington, DC: United States Conference of Catholic Bishops, 2006), 6.

22. Pope Francis, *The Name of God Is Mercy* (New York: Random House, 2016), 85.

23. Some of this section was previously published in the Boston College *Church in the 21st Century* magazine, Spring 2018.

24. I am indebted to the insights of my Buddhist colleague and author John Makransky for his work *Awakening through Love* (Wisdom Publications, 2007), from which these simplified versions of meditative prayer are adapted. Similar material was also first published by me in a blog post at https://www.ignatianspirituality.com/23734/resting-lords-gaze.

Bibliography

Battle, Michael. *Reconciliation: The Ubuntu Theology of Desmond Tutu*. Cleveland, OH: The Pilgrim Press, 1997.

Bethany House, ed. *Mirrors of Mercy*. Holts Summit, MO: Quail Valley Publishing, 2016.

Pope Francis. *The Church of Mercy: A Vision for the Church*. Chicago: Loyola Press, 2014.

Pope Francis. *The Name of God Is Mercy*. New York: Random House, 2016.

Grant, Robert. *The Way of the Wound: A Spirituality of Trauma and Transformation*. Oakland, CA: Robert Grant, 1999.

Griswold, Charles. *Forgiveness: A Philosophical Exploration*. New York: Cambridge University Press, 2007.

Hanh, Thich Nhat. *Thich Nhat Hanh: Essential Writings*. Edited by Robert Ellsberg. Maryknoll, NY: Orbis Books, 2001.

Harter, Michael, ed. *Hearts on Fire: Praying with the Jesuits*. Chicago: Loyola Press, 2005.

Himes, Michael. "Hope in a Wintry Season. " https://www.bc.edu/bc-web/schools/stm/sites/encore/main/2010/hope-wintery-season.html.

Ignatius of Loyola. *Spiritual Exercises and Selected Works*. Edited by George Ganss. Mahwah, NJ: Paulist Press, 1991.

Kaspar, Walter. *Mercy: The Essence of the Gospel and the Key to the Christian Life*. Mahwah, NJ: Paulist Press, 2014.

Makranksy, John. *Awakening through Love: Unveiling Your Deepest Goodness*. Boston: Wisdom Publications, 2007.

Nouwen, Henri. *The Return of the Prodigal Son: A Story of Homecoming*. New York: Doubleday, 1994.

Radcliffe, Timothy. *I Call You Friends*. London and New York: Continuum, 2012.

Rolheiser, Ronald. *The Holy Longing: The Search for a Christian Spirituality*. New York, Random House (Image Press), reissue edition, 2009.

Rupp, Joyce. *Praying Our Goodbyes*. New York: Ballantine, 1988.

Sacks, Jonathan. *To Heal a Fractured World: The Ethics of Responsibility*. New York: Schocken Books, 2005.

Salai, Sean. "The Psychological Insights of St. Ignatius of Loyola," *America Magazine*, August 6, 2018. https://www.americamagazine.org/faith/2018/08/06/psychological-insights-st-ignatius-loyola

Sotelo, Nicole. *Women Healing from Abuse: Meditations for Finding Peace*. Mahwah, NJ: Paulist Press, 2006.

Tobin, Eamon. *How to Forgive Yourself and Others: Steps to Reconciliation*. Liguori, MO: Liguori Publications, 2006.

Wolterstorff, Nicholas. "Jesus and Forgiveness" in *Jesus and Philosophy: New Essays*. Edited by Paul K. Moser. Cambridge: Cambridge University Press, 2008.

Acknowledgments

All good gifts come from God; I am grateful for how often the Spirit has spoken through the voices of other people in the course of my developing this book. So many people have contributed to the project directly or indirectly that it would be impossible to name them all. But I ought at least to make a beginning. Thank you to Clare Walsh, MHSH, and Judith Talvacchia, who were both gracious, patient, and talented teachers in the Boston College School of Theology and Ministry program for the training of spiritual directors. I first learned about the Spiritual Exercises from Brian Braman when he was the head of the BC Perspectives program, and from workshops with the late Howard Gray, SJ, who revitalized the Exercises and their place in the lives of many people. I am grateful to both of them and to Joe Appleyard, SJ, and

Julio Giulietti, SJ, who ran a seminar on Ignatian thought that I attended at BC.

A number of spiritual directors over the years, both at BC and at the Eastern Point Retreat House in Gloucester, Massachusetts, have offered me much wisdom; many ideas they offered me in the course of care for my own spiritual life have ended up in this book. Thanks especially to Sr. Margretta Flanagan, MFIC; Ken Hughes, SJ; Fred Maples, SJ; and Randy Sachs, SJ. I send my heartfelt thanks to Jack Butler, SJ, who opened the door to Ignatian spirituality for me; falling in love with Jesus through learning imaginative prayer has forever changed my life for the better, and I am grateful for all that I have learned from you. My sincere gratitude to John Murray, SJ, who first encouraged me to write about my spiritual experiences and also listened to so many of them. I would not have had the courage to write at all without this encouragement. Bill Barry, SJ, read some of my earliest essays on other topics in Ignatian spirituality and was generous enough to be honest with me about the initial shortcomings as well as the strengths, all with great kindness.

Thanks to Maria Cuadrado, Joe Durepos, and Vinita Hampton Wright, editors at Loyola Press who took a chance on my work and offered valuable advice on how to proceed with writing and rewriting. Denise Gorss has long been a valuable editor of my essays for the Ignatian Spirituality blog. Both Mary Troxell and Steve Pope read through the entire manuscript and offered generous and insightful comments on how to improve it. Friendships with Kerry Cronin, Todd Miller, Holly VandeWall, Julia Legas, Ashley Duggan, Serena Parekh, John Enslin, SJ, André Brouilllette, SJ, Eileen Sweeney, and so many others have sustained me on the road to reconciliation in my own life. Thanks for the laughter, listening, and for wiping away my tears. Students in the BC PULSE program continue to remind me of what it means to live mercy and justice. You continue to inspire me. Michael Boughton, SJ's homilies were just what I needed one year; thanks for saying the right things at the right times. Ruth Raichel has been not only a caring mentor but also the face of Christlike humility and gentleness. The men in the Lay Dominican Catholic group at MCI Norfolk prison have taught me so much about mercy and reconciliation; thank you for being such fine teachers to me. Last but not least, family is a schoolhouse for love; we learn how to forgive and be forgiven over and over again. Thanks to my parents, Maija and Valdis, my brother, Ray, for their constant support over the years. I wish to express gratitude for my late stepfather, Bill, and his encouragement of my work. Thanks to my husband, John, and my kids, Kay and Jim, for all the love, always.

About the Author

Marina McCoy is a professor of philosophy at Boston College who works on themes of vulnerability, rhetoric, and self-knowledge, among other topics. She is also a married mom of two adult children. Along with her teaching vocation, Marina enjoys volunteering at a men's prison, leading discussions of spirituality and accompanying others as a spiritual director.